# THE BUBBLE
# ECONOMY

# Christopher Wood

# THE BUBBLE ECONOMY

Japan's Extraordinary Speculative Boom of
the '80s and the Dramatic Bust of the '90s

THE ATLANTIC MONTHLY PRESS
NEW YORK

Published simultaneously in Canada
Printed in the United States of America


Library of Congress Cataloging-in-Publication Data

Wood, Christopher, 1944–
The bubble economy: Japan's extraordinary speculative boom of the
'80s and the dramatic bust of the '90s / Christopher Wood.
ISBN 0-87113-485-3
1. Stocks—Prices—Japan. 2. Speculation. 3. Stock-exchange—Japan.
4. Panics (Finance)—Japan. 5. Japan—Economic conditions—1945–1989.
6. Japan—Economic conditions—1989–
7. International finance. I. Title.
HG5773.W66   1992      332.63'222'0952—dc20      92-18432

The Atlantic Monthly Press
19 Union Square West
New York, NY 10003

FIRST PRINTING

To Kathleen, Justine, and Imogen

# ACKNOWLEDGMENTS

*The Bubble Economy* is the result of numerous conversations. Clearly it is impossible to name all the people who have given me ideas and inspiration. However, thanks are due in particular to my present employer, *The Economist*, for providing me with the opportunity to live in Japan during such interesting times. Naturally, all views expressed here are my own.

Thank you to Andrew Ballingal, Graeme McDonald, and Christofer Rathke for reading the raw manuscript and making many helpful suggestions. Thank you to Nicholas Valery for providing me with the clearest perspective on Japan—a beacon of rationality amid the baying camps of quislings and bashers. Thank you to Hiroko Ofuchi for all manner of practical help. Thank you to Morgan Entrekin, Takahisa Kimura, Jan Miller, William Miller, and Junzo Sawa for believing in the project. Finally, a special thank you to my family for putting up with the distraction of writing.

# CONTENTS

# 1

# Bubbles Do Matter

What everybody knows is seldom worth knowing. It is now fashionable to worry about the health of America's financial system. The problems in that country are at last obvious to nearly everyone: the savings and loan disaster, the worst property crash since the Great Depression, and the related crisis of bad debts ravaging the banking system itself. This concern is all quite proper, since America certainly suffers from an overdose of financial rot and empty buildings, but it needs to be asked how much of the mess has been taken into account by the market. The answer is a lot. America is an extraordinarily open society where the dirty linen is hung out for all to see. Very little is left to the imagination.

Where America is brutally transparent, Japan is devilishly opaque. It is harder for observers to discount what they do not know. As a result, the potential for the financial system to spring nasty surprises is now far greater in Japan than it is in America. Japan may have a first-rate economy that is the envy of the world, but it has a second-rate financial system. Leading Japanese financial institutions border on the feudal compared with their Western counterparts.

In the second half of the 1980s, Japan was involved in the biggest financial mania of this century, a boom that has now gone spectacularly bust. Japan will spend the first half of the 1990s working off the resulting excesses, a painful, contractional, time-consuming process that will inevitably reduce the country's capacity for economic growth. Recession in the form of slow or even negative economic growth now threatens the stability of Japan's post-1945 political order and has the potential to sink the world into a 1930s-style deflationary depression.

The Japanese like to refer to their speculative boom gone bust, fueled on cheap and supereasy credit, as the Bubble Economy. It is an apt description. The Bubble Economy inevitably spawned scandals in the banking and securities businesses, which had shocking consequences for the real economy. The Japanese have somehow managed to convince themselves that the Bubble Economy was a distinct and separate phenomenon from the real economy and therefore cannot damage it. This will prove an illusion.

Scandals are the inevitable consequence of any period of speculative excess. But Japan's scandals are more important than America's Ivan Boesky or Michael Milken cases or Britain's Guinness or Robert Maxwell affairs. The Western scandals may have brought down powerful figures and titillated the public with the spectacle of the superrich being carted off to jail (or worse in Maxwell's case), but they proved only of passing interest and did not cause lasting change. This will not be the case in Japan. During a few short months in the summer of 1991, a seemingly endless series of murky goings-on linking politics, finance, and the criminal underworld rocked the foundations of the Japanese establishment. Be it stockbrokers compensating favored investors for losses, securities companies financing attempts by organized crime to manipulate companies' stock, or bank managers fraudulently issuing billions of dollars worth of false certificates of deposit for use as phony collateral, the impression left by the constant drip of revelation was the same. Japan was wallowing in sleaze. The scandals, it seemed, were not isolated scams but systemic problems. Not even the venerated bureaucracy was immune. For the first time, many questioned publicly the morals of the Ministry of Finance, the country's most powerful institution, for seemingly being in bed with those it was supposed to regulate.

Many Japan experts, be they fervent admirers or hostile critics, dispute the assertion that the scandals will change anything. Their collective credo holds that nothing in Japan ever changes. They argue that a few months after the press has stopped writing about them, the scandals will be relegated to distant memory and Japan will be back to business as usual. What they ignore is that these scandals served both as symptoms of the greatest speculative fever seen this century and as warnings that that credit boom was about to implode. While Japan seems constant in many respects (after all, the Liberal Democrats have enjoyed a monopoly on political power since 1955), the 1980s brought electrifying changes. Under the prompting of foreign (mostly American) pressure, Japan began to deregulate much of its commercial life, freeing interest rates, lowering the duties on imported goods such as liquor, oranges, and beef, and liberalizing retail laws governing the establishment of supermarkets and convenience stores. Such changes may seem piecemeal, but they have already significantly improved the lot of the hard-toiling salaryman and the long-ripped-off consumer.

Still, there is plenty that needs changing. The Japanese will in future increasingly expect and demand of government more reform along these lines. This should be apparent to anyone living in Japan. The young and even the middle-aged are a quite different breed from their grandparents, who knew true deprivation and had to rebuild the country from the devastation of war. Young Japanese have a much better knowledge of the outside world. They are also more indulged and more spoiled. They are interested in leisure and consumption, and a whole range of service companies has sprouted up to fill their needs. This is only right and proper, an example of capitalism working as it is meant to when a country passes beyond a certain stage of economic development. Younger Japanese are even prepared to go into debt to indulge their whims, doubtless often to the consternation of their more conservative parents. Post-war Japan has for the most part remained a traditional cash-transaction society loyal to its agricultural roots where only companies, not respectable individuals, go into debt. Unauthorized overdrafts are more than frowned upon. If a check is bounced twice, the bank must still by law close down the bank account. Yet despite this thrifty culture, gross consumer debt soared to American levels in the 1980s. In the twelve years ending March 1991, consumer debt had exploded sevenfold, from ¥9 trillion at the end of 1979 to ¥67 trillion, according to figures released by Japan's official Economic Planning Agency. Per capita consumer debt was commensurate with America's by 1990: $2,985 in Japan against $2,915 in the United States.*

Japan is changing more than many foreign Japanese-speaking experts, with a huge vested professional interest in making the place seem more strange than it really is, are often prepared to acknowledge. The Japanese are not quite so weirdly different as the *gaijin* experts like to make out, though as an island nation they are undoubtedly fond of viewing themselves as a unique people living in a unique country. But then again, so are the British. The Japanese may appear "inscrutable orientals" to Western eyes, but it should always be remembered they fire off the same range of emotions as other people: greed, fear, shame, and honor.

This more human side, as opposed to the nightmare vision of an industrial army of toiling marcher ants conjured up in the rhetoric of protectionist politicians like former French prime minister Edith Cresson or Michigan congressmen, was on full public display during the scandals, warts and all. This was itself unusual in a society that almost cares more about form than substance. But the more significant point about these seedy affairs was that they revealed the degree of collusion within a corrupt establishment, an old-boy network characterized by cozy relations between politicians, bureaucrats, businessmen, financiers, and gangsters, in the context of Japan's greatest failure since 1945 and the launching of the economic miracle. That failure was a credit boom that was allowed to get dangerously and recklessly out of control and that has since gone spectacularly bust.

The Japanese are a pragmatic people. They have always been

---

*All exchange rates are at $1 = ¥133.

prepared to forgive their leaders in the post-1945 era because the system, blatantly venal and inequitable as it may be, delivered amazing results in terms of economic growth. No longer. At the end of the 1980s, Japan was basking in a collective self-confidence that too often bordered on arrogance. It will prove too fleeting a moment of superiority for a nation that, despite its wealth, still harbors deep feelings of insecurity.

Politically, Japan remains something of a eunuch, retaining an almost neocolonial dependence on America. It was America that set in motion the rebuilding of Japan after 1945 by surgically implanting a Western-style liberal democracy into a foreign host. It was the Americans who wrote the English-language constitution by which Japan is still governed, to the consternation of nationalist politicians like former prime minister Yasuhiro Nakasone. Even Japan's post-1945 prosperity has been built on extraordinarily generous access to America's consumer market, the world's largest. America was prepared to accord Japan this generosity because the country was its political ward and chosen ally in a hostile Asia dominated by communist China and Russia. During the cold war, the primacy of strategic interests over narrow economic ones made a lot of sense in Washington. It is precisely for this reason that, with the disappearance of the Soviet empire, Japan now finds much more being demanded of it by its chief ally. Witness the Americans' displeasure when the oil-dependent Japanese prevaricated for months over how to contribute to the Gulf War effort, a conflict about which Japan's leadership and most Japanese people felt ambivalent at best. Deep down they did not support the war, but in public they had to pretend they did. Their doubts reflected a discomfort with abstract principles of right and wrong and moral certitudes in general. Japan's ruling establishment could not conceive that America would actually follow through on its verbal threats and go to war over such an insignificant piece of territory as Kuwait. When war did break out, the Japanese were about the only people, apart from Saddam Hussein, to be genuinely surprised. When Japan finally agreed to contribute a total of $13 billion to the war effort, the nation and its taxpayers barely received a thank-you.

It was also made clear to the surprised Japanese that they would not benefit from the lucrative commercial contracts handed out for the reconstruction of Kuwait.

If the Japanese were still not politically self-confident at the end of the 1980s, that was far from the case in economics. This was quite natural, given Japan's extraordinary prowess in manufacturing and in the application of technology, best illustrated by its success in the automobile and consumer electronics industries. The virtues that made these triumphs possible included tremendous attention to detail and formidable powers of organization. However, the financial frenzy unleashed in the second half of the 1980s was so intense that its implosion now threatens that industrial prowess. The world has not yet understood this. The Tokyo stock market crash of 1990 was a painful jolt to the nation's collective self-confidence, to the sense of invincibility in matters economic. But as this book is written, the Japanese establishment still clings to the comforting though naive notion that the excesses of the Bubble Economy—the supposedly fringe world of the stock market, property market, and assorted speculative nonsense, such as frenzied trading in golf course memberships and the like—were somehow distinct and separate from the core industrial economy and therefore could not harm it. Unfortunately, this is not the case. Japanese industry was as much a beneficiary of the credit boom as the by-now discredited crooks and speculators; it too will be a victim of the bust. For example, between 1985 and 1990 Japanese companies raised some ¥85 trillion ($638 billion) through the stock market alone in what seemed at the time like virtually free financing. (A significant amount of it will probably turn out not to be so free, for reasons that will be explained later.) This was a colossal amount of money, much of which was used to finance Japan's biggest capital spending spree since 1945. If a portion of this expenditure must now be refinanced at much higher interest rates, it will inevitably hurt Japan's industrial competitiveness by raising companies' cost of capital.

Just as they like to dismiss the Bubble Economy as some sort of aberration grafted on to the "real" economy, the Japanese also

[6]

like to dismiss the astronomical values in their property market as essentially meaningless. The argument goes that property is seldom traded and therefore the values are not real. But a link between theoretical value and hard reality was eagerly provided during the bubble years by Japan's credit system and the pervasive use of land as collateral for credit. This makes everyone who has borrowed money using land as collateral, which is virtually everyone in Japan, vulnerable since property prices will suffer the same sort of crash as the Tokyo stock market, if not a more catastrophic one.

The bursting of the Bubble Economy has already laid to rest one myth, namely that Japanese stock prices always rise. It is in the process of demolishing another myth, namely that Japanese land prices cannot fall. The third myth, which will also soon be discredited, is the growth myth. The frantic economic growth of recent years based on a liquidity-triggered boom in private sector business investment is simply not sustainable. But this is to look ahead. It is worth remembering that as recently as the end of 1989, nearly all Japanese people—and many supposedly expert foreign observers peddling the "Japan is different" fallacy—viewed the explosion in asset prices in Japan during the previous five years as quite rational. It was the twentieth century's best example of the dictum of Charles Mackay, the celebrated nineteenth-century historian of speculative manias, who observed that men think in herds, go mad in herds, but only recover their senses one by one. As a group culture that discourages individualistic thinking, the Japanese are even more vulnerable than most to this decidedly human trait. The shock to their collective self-confidence has been immense.

Isaac Newton actually arrived in Japan in 1990. His presence did not prove a pretty sight in a country where too many people had concluded that the laws of gravity, when applied to their own financial markets, had somehow been suspended. Predictably, they had not. At its October 1, 1990, low Japan's Nikkei index had lost 48 percent of its value from its all-time high recorded, appropriately, on December 31, 1989, the final day of that fevered decade. At that bloated point of the bubble, the Japanese stock market had reached some staggering valuations. It represented 42 percent of the total capitalization of world stock markets, compared with only 15 percent in 1980, and it was worth 151 percent of Japan's gross national product, compared with just 29 percent in 1980. The crash from such dizzy heights was a shattering blow. It marked a decline in paper wealth of ¥300 trillion ($2.25 trillion), or more than four times the estimated thirty-year $500 billion cost of bailing out America's savings and loan industry and more than three times the size of the world's then-outstanding third world debt. It was also a much greater crash than the 36 percent decline suffered by America's Dow Jones Industrial Index in the memorable autumn of 1987. The New York Stock Exchange soon bounced back. The Tokyo Stock Exchange did not. At the beginning of 1992, the Japanese stock market remained stuck in the doldrums, some 45 percent off its all-time highs.

Amid this financial debris there remained the continuing anomaly of Japan's extraordinary land bubble. Japan's total stock of property was still valued in 1990 at a theoretical ¥2,000 trillion, or five times the size of Japan's gross national product and some four times the value of the total stock of property in America. The threat was clear. Any decline in that market similar to what had befallen Japan's stock market would mean a plunge in the value of the collateral held by those institutions, principally Japanese banks, that had lent so freely against land. Since they are also the world's biggest commercial banks, accounting for nearly 40 percent of all international cross-border lending, that would further accelerate the contraction in the availability of Japanese credit worldwide that the Japanese stock market crash had already started. All this occurred at a time when America's banking system, the world's second biggest, was already in the midst of its own crisis and resulting credit contraction, the worst since the 1930s, as it struggled under the crushing weight of an epidemic of bad debts, most of them property related. With Germany preoccupied with financing the huge and unpredictable costs of taking over its former communist half and with the former Soviet empire in a state of near anarchy, there were no obvious candidates left to take up the slack and stimulate world economic activity.

[8]

Developments in Japanese finance could no longer only be considered in terms of their consequences inside Japan. The numbers had become too big, the credit binge too extreme for that. As the marginal supplier of that extra dollar of credit, as the lender and purchaser of frequent resort, Japan supported asset markets throughout the world during the 1980s, be they financial assets like American Treasury bonds or physical assets like London and Los Angeles office buildings or French Impressionist paintings.

The turning off of that hose of liquidity and the resulting intensifying global credit squeeze raised the specter of worldwide deflation, when debts go bad and money supply contracts. The last time the world suffered such a misfortune was during the 1930s, after the financial markets of America, then the major creditor nation, went into a tailspin. The same warning flag was raised by Japan's stock market crash in 1990. Professional moneymen suddenly began to embrace the apocalyptic view, using arguments that they had earlier derided as being peddled only by perverse mavericks or mystic cranks. There was open talk of the risk of a financial crisis and worldwide debt defaults. This unmentionable-no-longer is indeed what is at stake. For a full-scale crash in Japan will make America's current deflationary downturn look like a picnic. It will also exacerbate and prolong it.

The unpleasantness will take several forms. The Nikkei index could fall far lower than any conventional pundit currently expects—perhaps to 12,000, at which point the capital gains on the huge stock portfolios of the banks and life insurance companies will be wiped out. Such a drop would mark a 70 percent decline from the market's top, which is not so farfetched, given the extreme overvaluations reached at the height of the Tokyo bull market. After all, Taiwan's stock market fell in 1990 by 80 percent from top to bottom. Japan's liquidity bubble was almost as great as Taiwan's, and its financial-services sector almost as primitive. In fact, 12,000 is a good target for the Nikkei, though the stock market would even then be a long way from a screaming bargain. John Bolsover, chief executive of London-based Baring Asset Management, explained why in a speech delivered on October 19, 1991. Bolsover quoted an old Japanese rice traders' saying: *"Han ne hachi gake ni wari biki.*" Loosely translated, this means that it is only safe to buy when a market has halved and the would-be buyer takes 80 percent of that figure and then a 20 percent discount. Applying that rule to the Nikkei would imply a level of 12,453, which would still put the stock market, according to Bolsover, on a far from cheap price-earnings ratio of 23 and a dividend yield of 1.2 percent.

An even more traumatic crash in the Japanese stock market is only one form of nastiness to be expected. Another unpleasant surprise will be an equally severe crash in land prices. This will be more devastating to a nation and a banking system that never conceived that the value of land could implode and that therefore placed far too much faith in it as a store of value for use as collateral. The land disaster will trigger bank failures, forcing taxpayer bailouts. It will precipitate a fire sale of the overseas assets of the big money-center banks (known as "city" banks) to shore up their shrunken capital at home. The impact of the resulting decline in bank shares will devastate the rest of the stock market, since the banks represent one quarter of that market. There is plenty of room to fall. Bolsover pinpointed in his speech the absurdity of a situation where the blue-chip Industrial Bank of Japan (IBJ) is valued by the Tokyo stock market at $63 billion, whereas Wall Street's premier investment bank Morgan Stanley (whose profits are only 40 percent less than IBJ's declared profits) is valued at $3.6 billion. Bolsover added that the impact of this decline in bank shares on Japan's system of cross-shareholdings (where companies hold shares in one another as a way of consolidating long-term relationships) "scarcely bears thinking about as the cross-holdings so recently held up as a virtue become unwound." These cross-shareholdings will indeed become victims of the burst bubble as many of the many Japanese companies that own bank shares decide to sell them. In addition, Japan's giant life insurance companies will no longer be able to meet their obligations out of cash flow.

These traumas will, fortunately, have a cathartic effect. They will accelerate the development of a modern financial marketplace in Japan as the ravages of debt deflation sweep away the feudal cobwebs. In the future, capital will be allocated more efficiently in Japan, no longer on the basis of who knows whom. The much talked about potential for mergers and acquisitions will also be fulfilled, but in the opposite direction from what most of Tokyo's underemployed investment bankers now expect. Instead of Japanese entities buying American or European companies, American and European companies will have the opportunity to buy Japanese assets on the cheap.

The causes of the bursting of the biggest speculative bubble seen this century can only be found in the idiosyncrasies of Japan's long-regulated, long-cosseted, and highly cartelized financial sector. While Japan has a superefficient manufacturing sector of which it can be justly proud, its financial sector can make no such boasts. Leading Japanese financial institutions are primitive, which is why they were so ill prepared for the two trends that so abruptly ended the financial mania in Tokyo. The first was the doubling of interest rates between early 1989 and late 1990 engineered by a central bank finally determined to burst a dangerously bloated speculative bubble. The second was the phased deregulation of Japan's financial system, largely in response to foreign pressure.

Many intelligent Westerners, who should have known better, became adept at inventing semiplausible rationalizations of the astronomic price-earnings ratios that became commonplace in the Tokyo stock market during the second half of the 1980s and that reached their extreme when the shares of Nippon Telegraph and Telephone, the public telephone monopoly, were floated on the Tokyo stock market by a greedy Japanese government at a price-earnings ratio of 250. The many small retail investors who bought them saw the value of their holdings decline by some 80 percent over three years. Among the reasons cited for Tokyo's lofty price-earnings ratios were the peculiarities of Japan's accounting system and the country's cross-shareholding system, as a result of which more than 60 percent of shares owned are never traded. Such self-serving explanations performed the practical service of allowing professional investors to keep rationalizing a liquidity-driven boom. This helped keep the stock market rolling and stockbroking commissions pouring in long after the worldwide October 1987 crash had sounded an ominous warning about the nature of the debt-financed prosperity of the 1980s and put a permanent dent in the trading volumes of most of the world's other major stock markets.

However, these explanations ignored the real reason for Japan's sky-high stock prices: the country's prolonged period of low interest rates. Between January 1986 and February 1987, the Bank of Japan, the central bank, lowered the official discount rate from 5 percent to 2.5 percent. As a consequence, bank loans were available for as little as 4 percent to their best corporate customers. Even better than that, publicly quoted companies could exploit a rising stock market by raising money using the neat trick of issuing Eurobonds with warrants attached in London's offshore Euromarket, the world's largest debt market, and swapping the dollar exposure back into yen. Money became virtually free in Japan. This sparked a liquidity boom to beat all others. At its center lay the economy's main engine of credit creation, the banks. They were able to use a rising stock market literally to create bank capital and thus boost their lending. That extra credit was funneled back into two main markets (shares and property), boosting the value of banks' favored collateral (shares and property) against which to lend still more money.

The game is now over for good. This is beginning to be understood by the leaders of Tokyo's financial community, but the contractional consequences have yet to be grasped fully in groupthink Japan, where the consensus is always supposed to be right. Instead of responding to adversity, meeting the challenge, and moving on, senior managers in Japan's financial institutions are more like frightened rabbits caught at night in a car's headlights. Confronted by the unfamiliar and used to being told what to do by the overweening Ministry of Finance, they are frozen into inaction. Not knowing how to respond, they have decided to do nothing, hanging on in the forlorn hope that the problem will go away. This is the worst of all responses.

Take the reaction of Japan's stockbroking community to the 1990 crash. This was compared by Deryck Maughan, then the boss of investment bank Salomon Brothers' Tokyo office and now the New York–based president of Salomon Incorporated, to that of a punch-drunk heavyweight boxer who keeps picking himself up from the floor at the count of nine only to be knocked down again. Thus once-mighty Nomura, Japan and the world's biggest stock-broking firm, saw its stock market worth plunge by more than $50 billion from its peak in 1987 even before its chairman and president were forced to resign as a result of scandals in the summer of 1991. During 1990 Nomura's Tokyo pundits, like those of every other Japanese securities firm and many foreign securities firms, wrongly called the bottom of the stock market numerous times. Their problem was that they could not take a pessimistic view, since the Japanese stock market is not supposed to go down. During the downturn, Japanese stockbrokers were resigning or not show-ing up for work. They could no longer stand the dishonor of having to talk to their increasing fed-up clients.

This demoralization matters because it can become self-feed-ing. In a consensus society where there are few contrarians, yester-day's collective euphoria can too easily degenerate into tomorrow's collective panic. So far the signs are mixed. The plunging stock market instilled a certain sense of panic into even the mightiest institutions, yet there has remained an apparent confidence that land prices will decline, at worst, by an orderly 30 percent and that the still seemingly strong economy will keep growing, albeit at a slower and therefore more sustainable pace.

This outcome may be theoretically possible. But it presup-poses that a speculative bubble can be burst without causing a string of nasty financial accidents that feed into the real economy; that greed can revert to sobriety without a bout of panic. The point is that it is comparatively easy to predict financial crises. The hard part is getting the timing and magnitude right. (Witness America's savings and loan mess.)

It seems far more likely that Japan will instead suffer a vicious credit squeeze of a kind not seen since 1945. This contraction will have three causes: first, the dramatic surge in industry's cost of capital after so many years of enjoying the free ride of ultralow interest rates; second, the stock market's collapse and its shrinking effect on bank lending; and third, a banking crisis caused by an avalanche of bad debts, most of them property related. The effects of this contraction will be felt worldwide. The question is how Japan's once-respected financial bureaucrats will cope with this challenge. Japan as a society has a tremendous record for pulling together in a crisis, as opposed to the dog-eat-dog behavior normal in Anglo-Saxon countries. A proud example of Japan's strength is that no Japanese bank has been allowed to fail since 1945. This strength is usually attributed to the power wielded by the government bureaucracy, which still employs much of Japan's best talent. It also explains why most people remain so confident that Japan's manufacturing economy will survive the current financial problems virtually unscathed.

There is one problem with this comforting argument. Deregulation may have broken down the communality of interest that has been such an important part of financial stability in Japan. By reluctantly allowing deregulation of bank deposit rates at the demand of American trade negotiators, officials at the revered Ministry of Finance may have improved the lot of the individual saver. But in the process they have also hugely reduced their own power to control events. In a deregulated financial world, what counts is who can raise capital cheapest, not who has best access to the bureaucrats.

Gloomy forecasts about Japan will appear absurd to many. It is certainly true that Japan still enjoys some major strengths, of which the greatest are the accumulated personal savings of its citizens, the quality of its industrial infrastructure, and the discipline and industry of its work force. Proof that the more human of these qualities were not suddenly discovered in the 1960s by prescient management gurus or smart investment managers is clear from a book written in 1905 by the British political journalist Alfred Stead entitled *Great Japan: A Study in National Efficiency.* This was published at a time when the British, like the Americans today, were obsessed by the subject of their own industrial decline. The book included a preface by Lord Rosebery, a British prime minister, in which he wrote, "Japan is indeed the object-lesson of national efficiency, and happy is the country that learns it."

Japan's strengths are indeed formidable and should not be underestimated, but they do not preclude the Japanese economy from suffering the ravages of debt deflation (the American economy was already the world's largest in the late 1920s, but it still was rocked by the Great Depression). In fact, Japan is not quite as cash rich and debt free as most people think. Far from it. America's nonfinancial debt during the 1980s rose from 140 percent to 185 percent of its gross national product (GNP). Though it was ignored by most economists at the time, it is this debt load that has so far prevented America from staging a robust recovery in the 1990s. Yet in Japan, total private sector nonfinancial debt was a much greater 277 percent of Japan's GNP as of March 31, 1989, according to the most recent data published by the official Economic Planning Agency. This reflects in large part the sea of debt underpinning land prices. It is this bubble that makes Japan the most vulnerable of the world's major economies to a credit deflation. The two sectors most vulnerable to such a deflation, namely financial services and property, account for 16 percent of Japan's GNP. With capital spending still representing 23 percent of Japan's GNP at the end of 1991, the potential for Japan's boom to bust rather more painfully than the vast majority of economists expect becomes obvious.

Such thoughts were not on most Americans' minds at the beginning of 1992. Instead of understanding Japan's vulnerability, reflected in the doldrums of the Tokyo stock market and the precarious condition of the country's banks, many Americans had convinced themselves that Japan was the enemy and America its victim, stuck in a permanent decline. Yet Wall Street was making new all-time highs despite the continuing recession. One reason for this American reaction is the exaggerated attention paid by the politicians and the media to the perceived threat of Japan, symbolized by its trade surplus with America. Yet the trade problem was exaggerated. True, Japan's current account surplus in 1991 totaled $72.1 billion, not so far off the peak figure of $85.8 billion reached in 1986. But the two main reasons for this had nothing to do with America. First, imports into Japan were down both because of slumping domestic demand in a weakening economy and because Japan was spending much less on vital imports like oil because these commodities were so much cheaper in the deflationary 1990s. Second, Japan's trade surplus with Europe had grown. In the first six months of 1991 Japan's merchandise trade surplus with the European Economic Community was $16.3 billion, nearly double the level of 1986. By comparison, the merchandise trade surplus was $18.5 billion with America in the same period and $20.9 billion with the rest of Asia. By focusing on the nominal figures alone, it was easy to miss the extent to which Japan's current account surplus had declined in the context of its overall economy. The current account surplus was 4.3 percent of GNP in 1986. By 1991 the figure had shrunk to 2.2 percent. By listening to bad advice and taking the heads of the three Detroit carmakers (against their better judgment) to Tokyo with him in early January 1992, President George Bush did a disservice to everyone, but most of all to himself. By adopting the unfamiliar role of car salesman he chose to identify himself with perhaps America's biggest industrial failure. Yet there was an American success story to boast about in manufactured exports. America has increased its share of the Organization for Economic Cooperation and Development's manufactured exports from 14 percent in 1987 to an estimated 18 percent in 1991.

Bush's clumsy attempt at political expediency embarrassed more than angered a Japanese leadership that was sensitive to his political problems at home. But the president's actions and even some of his rhetoric seemed to concede the trade argument to the vociferous lobby of protectionist-inclined Japan bashers in America. The perennial trade argument with Japan has been simmering for years, but the confrontations have for the most part been semiritualistic and without real bile. But with the end of the cold war and with its middle class mired in the worst downturn since the 1930s, America needed a new enemy. Bush's irresponsible actions helped relations between America and Japan take on an ugly new note with barely concealed racial overtones. Forgotten was the fact that Japanese direct investments in America, actively sought by state governments, had created numerous jobs; forgotten was the fact that America's property slump would have been that much worse had Japanese buyers not been on hand to pay top dollar prices for so many assets. Japanese owners of property in Japan must now wish they could be so lucky.

American criticism of Japan, and Detroit's special pleading, became so irrational that the Japanese could no longer tolerate it in silence. On January 27, Yutaka Kume, president of Nissan, Japan's second-largest carmaker, took the unusual step of calling in the Tokyo correspondents of America's major newspapers to issue a strongly worded criticism of Detroit. The Japanese reaction was both understandable and justified. They had not forced American consumers to favor Japanese cars over the homemade variety. But the fact that Kume's response was considered a big deal at the time only underlines how publicly restrained the Japanese have been in withstanding American attacks. The Japanese have for the most part chosen to remain silent not because they are nice guys but because they understand where their interests lie. Japan still needs America, in particular access to its enormous consumer market, far more than America needs Japan. America has a huge continental economy that can ignore trade if it really has to. It can also fund its budget deficit internally if the Japanese decided to sell all their holdings of American Treasury bonds. The worst that would happen is that long-term interest rates would rise by a few basis points (hundredths of a percentage point). In contrast, Japan has to export to pay for its imported natural resources, of which oil is only one example out of many. It is also dependent on American military might to safeguard the shipping routes on which these resources are transported. This is not a relationship in which Japan has the upper hand.

The Bubble Economy needs to be seen in the context of this vulnerability and the risks posed to Japan by the deteriorating relationship with America. The Bubble Economy represents the most dramatic failure of post-1945 Japanese economic management. The shocks and general upheaval predicted in this book have the potential to undermine both Japan's existing political order and the confidence of its bureaucracy and business community in continued economic growth. This is not to say that the Japanese economy is finished; that would be absurd. But the immediate future is far bleaker than most suppose.

There are those who will contend that this view is much too gloomy, that Japan has consistently made fools of those who predict problems for it. They will say that Japan's bureaucrats will always be able to stave off financial collapse by changing the rules of the game whenever it is deemed necessary. The belief in the power of administrators is as seductively convincing as it is wrong, since it is based on the extraordinary premise that Japan is somehow immune from the laws of economics and the cyclical whims of markets. Japan's managed economy may delay the impact of market forces, but it can never repeal them. It is worrying that the bureaucrats think that they are in charge, that they can control the inevitable fallout from deregulation by habitual behind-the-scenes weaving and dodging. True, they will be able to manage the first few "crises" and initially avoid the embarrassment of small banks going bust or property companies dumping land on the market. However, once problems become more systemic, it will be increasingly hard for officials to control events in the traditional ad hoc manner because there will by then be too many fires to put out. Even Japanese pragmatism has its limits. As for the Ministry of Finance, it is about to enter a middle-aged crisis as Japan's financial-services sector grows up and the ministry's own powers wane, leaving it a relic of the displaced *ancien régime*.

There is another danger. Like America, Japan has its own sort of moral hazard problem. The vast majority of people active in Japanese finance or commerce, including most foreigners, still subscribe to the notion that Japan Inc. will never let financial institutions go bust, that all credits are good, and that all deposits are safe. As in federally insured America, this reassuring belief in the system's underwriting of all sorts of credit risk has itself amplified the speculative bubble. It also raises the danger of great disappointment or worse should this widely shared conviction ever be challenged. For in a consensus society, the longer the suspension of reality, the greater the potential for panic when everyone suddenly changes their minds. This extreme outcome cannot be dismissed out of hand, since the level of speculation witnessed in Japan in recent years was itself extreme and therefore does not lend itself to mild corrections.

In the short term there is no way out for Japan, which now faces the sort of hangover appropriate after such a long and feverish party. Such a financial mania could never have occurred if Japan had not achieved a certain level of prosperity. But that prosperity had almost everything to do with the commercial abilities of Japan's exporters and the savings accumulated by its hard-working labor force and almost nothing to do with the skills of its financial-services sector. Sadly, much of that hard-won wealth will now be destroyed far more quickly than it was ever created.

But before describing the pain of the bust, it is necessary to recount briefly the origins of the boom, to examine how it began and why it was allowed to get so out of control. The Bubble Economy has its origins in misguided efforts at international economic diplomacy, efforts on which the major international powers are now increasingly turning their backs as they pursue their own domestic agendas. The key starting point was September 1985's Plaza Accord, the international agreement to drive down the value of the dollar and so help reduce America's huge trade deficits with both Japan and Germany. Although they did not quite appreciate it at the time, the world's leading governments had in fact decided to knock a currency that had already begun to correct from a period of gross overvaluation. The heavy hand of Plaza was to turn that decline into a rout. By the Louvre Accord of February 1987, the priorities had reversed. The dollar had collapsed, putting unprecedented pressure on Japanese and German exporters and causing a slowdown in their export-dependent economies. The Americans used bullyboy tactics at the Louvre meeting, threatening further dollar weakness (Washington has always shown an extraordinary lack of concern about talking down its own currency to the impoverishment of Americans) to get the Japanese and Germans to loosen their own monetary policy.

The Bank of Japan responded much more readily to this pressure than the far more independent Bundesbank. America made clumsy efforts later that year to jawbone the Germans into monetary easing (which frightened the financial markets and served as the immediate catalyst of the October 1987 crash, an event that terrified officialdom, as well as investors). But the Japanese had needed no such cajoling. As part of the Louvre Accord the Bank of Japan lowered the official discount rate in February to 2.5 percent, its lowest level in the postwar period. This sowed the seeds for the supereasy credit that led to the Bubble Economy. To be fair to the Japanese central bank, that final easing in monetary policy was not solely triggered by American pressure. Japan in 1986 was mired in a Japanese-style recession (economic growth of only 2.6 percent) caused by the problems confronting the export sector as a result of the yen's sharp appreciation. This still seemed to be the case to the Bank of Japan in early 1987, even though in hindsight it became clear that the trough of the business downturn was reached in November 1986. But in easing once again, the central bank underestimated fatally, as bureaucrats tend to, the animal spirits unleashed within the domestic economy by an abundance of cheap credit. The result was a domestic boom to beat all booms, but one distorted fatally by the peculiarities of Japan's banking system and the archaic laws governing the country's property market. The Bubble Economy had begun.

# 2

# Banks

Japan's banks may be the world's largest in terms of assets, but their commercial prowess does not match their size. Profoundly conservative hierarchical institutions locked into rigid business relationships, the banks smack of a former, more authoritarian era. Senior bank management has traditionally looked for guidance from its mentors, the Ministry of Finance and its mandarins, and like a young adult reluctant to leave home, finds the habit hard to buck. Bank employees are taught to obey orders blindly rather than come up with ideas of their own. Initiative is almost positively discouraged. This culture made the banks peculiarly ill suited to cope with the wrenching change posed by deregulation of interest rates. The result has been predictably disastrous.

Historians may well conclude that the post-1945 era in Japanese banking ended with the sudden resignation on October 8, 1990, of the chairman of Sumitomo Bank, Ichiro Isoda. Isoda stepped down to take responsibility for the misdeeds of a branch manager who allegedly persuaded Sumitomo clients to lend ¥23 billion to a group of stock market speculators to conduct a share ramp (the organized manipulation of a share price). The offense was not as important as the blow to the prestige of the man and of the institution in a financial system where, until the epidemic of scandals that would break out several months later, skeletons usually remained firmly locked in closets unless criminal charges were made and public disclosure became obligatory. Isoda was both the grand old man of Japanese banking and the long-term authoritarian ruler of Sumitomo; Sumitomo was considered the most aggressive and innovative of Japan's big city banks in the 1980s, the equivalent of America's Citicorp. Isoda's resignation confirmed growing suspicions that Japan's banks, Sumitomo in particular, had been fanning an orgy of speculation in the stock and property markets and that Sumitomo's acclaimed "aggression," like Citicorp's, was really no more than a polite way of saying that the bank had made lots of unwise loans to lots of unsound people and would end up losing lots of money.

That Japan's banks have lent heavily against both property and shares in recent years is not in doubt. At the end of June 1991, a total of ¥116 trillion had been lent directly to the property and construction sectors. City banks' outstanding domestic loans, collateralized by land, stand at about 50 percent of Japan's GNP. In the boom years of 1987 and 1988, loans collateralized by property accounted for more than half of city banks' incremental loan growth. That growth has since come to a grinding halt because of the Tokyo stock market crash and tougher international capital-adequacy standards for banks. These factors will combine to precipitate, at best, a shakeout and subsequent consolidation in Japanese banking. At worst, it will produce a wave of bank failures. They also explain why Japan began to suffer the first traumas of an American-style credit crunch in 1991 as banks' loan growth turned virtually flat. In 1990, interest rates surged in Japan as borrowers competed for funds in a white-hot economy. By the end of 1991 needy borrowers competed for a reduced supply of credit as bankers pulled in their horns, just as beleaguered banks had already done in America, fearing credit risk.

The nub of the Japanese banks' problem is that the conditions that let them boost their lending so dramatically during the 1980s have now reversed. City banks' assets increased by 80 percent between 1985 and 1989 as Japan binged on credit, yet despite ample warning, the banks were singularly ill prepared for the collapse of this peculiarly bloated credit pyramid.

Japanese banks have to contend with two long-term trends to which they have had plenty of time to adapt. First, they can no longer count on lending to their traditional customers, the large cash-rich companies that are the blue chips of industrial Japan. Such companies now raise money more cheaply by selling securities in the international capital markets. As a result, banks have lent increasingly in recent years to medium and small companies and to consumers, mainly in the form of mortgages. This is a largely rational response to the loss of their traditional corporate market. Unfortunately, many of these loans are backed by property.

The second trend is a sea change in the cost of the banks' deposits caused by deregulation of interest rates. Predictably, the Japanese finance ministry gave its charges, the banks, several years to prepare for this momentous transition. Deregulation of interest rates began in earnest in 1985 and was not completed until April 1991, when all deposits over ¥500,000 began to earn money-market rates. However, the banks chose not to respond to this dramatic increase in their funding costs in a rational commercial manner by passing on the cost to borrowers by charging them more. Instead, they ignored the blow to their profitability and kept on pursuing asset growth in order to boost their share of the market. They were able to do this only because of the buoyant Tokyo stock market. As more and more of their deposits were deregulated, banks filled the widening hole in their operating profits by recording capital gains from the sales of stocks held in their huge portfolios. The extent to which this went on during the late 1980s' bull market was truly remarkable. In the financial year ending on March 31, 1989, an average of 42 percent of the reported profits of Japan's city banks came from securities gains. Dai-Ichi Kangyo Bank, Japan's largest, realized 60 percent of its profits from selling shares. A study carried out by the Tokyo office of McKinsey, probably the world's premier management consulting firm, shows the extent to which this practice distorted banks' profits. Between 1984 and 1990, Japanese banks reported an average annual profit increase of 13 percent. However, if profits from the sales of long-term shareholdings and short-term stock market deals are excluded,

McKinsey calculated that the annual average increase in profit earned by the banks on their underlying business was only 1 percent. This is a pathetic performance considering the banks were enjoying booming asset growth at the time.

The trouble with these profits from sales of securities is not only that they were one-off extraordinary gains, but also that these transactions were mere paper shuffling. The banks generated no extra cash, and therefore no real profit. Even though the banks made big taxable profits on the sale of the shares that they may have owned for many years, they immediately had to buy back the same shares at prevailing bull market prices. The banks were obliged to do this under Japan's *keiretsu* system of cross-shareholdings, where financial institutions and industrial groups own one another's shares as a way of consolidating long-term business relationships. This was precisely the reason the banks had large share portfolios in the first place. These cross-shareholdings still account for more than 60 percent of the Tokyo stock market's shrunken capitalization.

Such paper shuffling had two nasty consequences. First, the banks may have booked a paper profit, but they took a loss in cash terms, since they had to pay tax on the capital gain, though they had repurchased the shares they had sold. Second, by selling the shares and then buying them back, they raised the average cost of their shareholdings. This did not matter terribly when the stock market was booming; now it matters a lot. Mikuni and Company, Japan's only independent bank credit-rating agency, reckons that all the city banks' capital gains on their share portfolios would be wiped out if the Nikkei declined to 13,000. This is a conservative estimate.

This mutual back-scratching system of cross-shareholdings (I buy your share if you buy mine) may make some sense in cementing business relationships. But it caused Japan's banks to make the mistake of assuming it would be easy for them to meet new capital-adequacy standards agreed to by the Basel-based Bank for International Settlements (BIS), which stipulate that international banks should have capital equal to at least 8 percent of their assets (once those assets have been weighted according to their riskiness) by a deadline (in Japan's case) of March 1993. These rules may sound rather technical, but they need to be explained in some detail because they are key to understanding not only Japanese banks' vulnerability but also the fragility of Japan's financial system itself. The banks are pivotal to the Japanese economy, and they are the country's main engine of credit creation to a far greater extent than is the case in America. Banks account for a far greater proportion of total credit extended in Japan than in America, a country with far more sophisticated capital markets and therefore more financing options available to borrowers. Bank loans equaled 90 percent of nominal GNP at the end of September 1991 in Japan, compared with 37 percent in America. The importance of the banks explains why BIS has become almost a household term in Japan. Under BIS rules, capital consists of so-called tier-one capital (which is real equity, consisting of shareholders' funds and retained earnings) and tier-two capital (which is anything else that can be counted, including loan-loss reserves, subordinated debt, and "hidden" assets). For Japan's banks, such "hidden" assets are 45 percent of the unrealized gains on stock holdings. However, to make the 8 percent ratio, at least half of that 8 percent must count as tier-one capital.

To allow banks to use any of their unrealized share gains as capital was always a controversial point in the BIS discussions. The Bank of England, for example, was firmly opposed for sound prudential reasons; after all, stock prices go down as well as up. In the end, as so often happens, an unsatisfactory compromise was reached. The Japanese banks were allowed to count 45 percent of their unrealized stock gains toward their capital. That fudge has proved a decidedly mixed blessing. It gave the banks leeway to go on acting irrationally by not passing the cost of deregulated interest rates on to their borrowers, with the resulting adverse impact on their own underlying profitability. But even more important, it made the banks' capital dependent on the fluctuations of the Tokyo stock market. This is the fatal flaw of Japan's financial system. The capital of the world's biggest banks, and therefore their ability to lend, goes up and down with the short-term whims

them to reduce their loan growth anyway. In fact, the central bank's strictures gave them a convenient excuse to say no to would-be borrowers or to charge them more.

By the end of 1991, the contraction of Japanese credit had become obvious, most clearly to cash-strapped borrowers. The process of shrinking actually began outside Japan. The banks began to sell off their assets overseas, where they had expanded hugely in recent years in pursuit of often miserably thin profit margins. There was lots of room for pruning. In the past ten years, the city banks expanded their overseas assets by nearly 25 percent annually in yen terms. Overseas assets accounted for nearly one-half of the major banks' total assets at the end of 1990, but these assets earned net lending spreads less than one-tenth of those achieved at home.

This overseas expansion was funded in a fundamentally risky way. Because Japanese banks do not have a foreign branch network taking in retail deposits, they resorted to the favored practice of the financially reckless since time immemorial. They borrowed short to lend long. The chosen vehicle was the London-based offshore Euromarkets, the world's dominant debt market. This raises the risk of a liquidity panic occurring in the interbank market triggered by some sort of financial accident in Japan, since Japanese banks have to rotate their financial liabilities constantly to fund those overseas assets, and the sums involved are not small. The Japanese banks had borrowed some ¥186 trillion offshore by the end of June 1990, according to Bank of Japan figures. About ¥69 trillion, or 37 percent, of this sum had been lent out. The Japanese banks were not worried because of the comfort provided by their "hidden" reserves. But as the falling Tokyo stock market eroded those capital gains during 1990, the rate they had to pay to borrow offshore rose. Japanese banks, despite being the world's largest, found themselves having to pay a premium, the so-called Japan rate, for their deposits, just as some of the beleaguered New York money-center banks like Citicorp and Chase Manhattan, weighed down by a torrent of property loans gone bad, have had to in order to satisfy nervous lenders.

The Japanese banks did not always lend the offshore funds wisely. Where they have ventured into higher-yielding assets they have often come unstuck. They are reckoned to have lent between $30 and $40 billion to fund American leveraged buyouts (LBOs). Their exposure to bought-out companies that are not paying interest has been estimated at some $4 billion. And as they had done at home, the Japanese banks piled into property lending overseas.

The Japanese banks lent big in America, mainly California. They owned 12.4 percent of total American banking assets at the end of June 1990, a share that amounted to $408 billion. In California they accounted for 24.5 percent of all bank assets at the end of June 1991. Japanese-owned banks owned 35 percent of all commercial and industrial loans in the state and 20 percent of all property loans. The latter figure might seem comparatively low, but it was double the share of property loans held by Japan in 1986. The Japanese did most of their lending at the peak of the market. California's property market has slumped badly since 1990 in a recession that by some estimates had cost that former go-go state 400,000 jobs by the end of 1991.

These market-share figures included assets held both by the Japanese banks' American branches and agencies and by the Japanese banks' American subsidiaries. The Japanese own the fifth, sixth, and seventh largest banks in California: in order of size, Union Bank (owned by the Bank of Tokyo), the Bank of California (owned by Mitsubishi Bank), and Sanwa Bank of California (owned by Sanwa Bank). To date attention has mainly focused on the loan problems faced by these American subsidiaries because of California's deteriorating property market. Their troubles are more visible because, as American corporate entities, they report their results separately, whereas agencies and branches are consolidated into the Japanese parent banks' results. Thus, Mitsubishi Bank in 1991 had to inject $250 million into the Bank of California to cover rising loan-loss provisions. This San Francisco–based bank also sacked hundreds of employees, a first for a Japanese-owned bank in America, though Sanwa California is poised to do the same. Even Union Bank, which traditionally has been more conservative in credit matters, announced in September 1991 a $90 million provision for loan losses.

These problems are comparatively minor compared with the

bad loans piling up in the American agencies and branches of the major Japanese banks. These divisions have much larger credit problems. Traditionally, they functioned as service centers for Japanese companies operating in America. That role changed dramatically in the mid-1980s as the Japanese banks began booking assets abroad frantically at "infinitessimal margins," according to management consultants familiar with their activities. The American branches earned a puny return on equity of about 2 percent, way below their cost of borrowing dollars in the Euromarkets. A 15 percent return on equity would be a more respectable target for this sort of wholesale banking.

The Japanese foreign-lending frenzy peaked at the same time as American property prices. In the financial year ended March 1990 the city banks Mitsui Taiyo Kobe and Mitsubishi Bank increased the value of their international loans by 45 percent and 37 percent respectively, while their domestic loans rose only 11 percent. Big-ticket loan syndications on office buildings and hotels were a favored vehicle, though the Japanese banks were also attracted to the hefty up-front fees available in leveraged buyout lending. Japanese banks provided almost 40 percent of the financing for the $25 billion RJR Nabisco buyout. Note that the Japanese banks brought no comparative advantage to the table aside from their funding ability. Their American branches tended to be staffed, to quote one New York–based management consultant, "by Japanese executives on a two-year rotation from Tokyo and by fourth-rate Americans," while the credit decisions were usually made back in Tokyo, where there was scant knowledge of America's local property markets. The Japanese banks tended to lend together, doubtless gaining comfort in numbers.

The downtown Los Angeles office market is symbolic of the Japanese banks' credit problems in America. The Japanese financed virtually every new building in the city. The multitude of half-empty skyscrapers gives Los Angeles an eerie, almost surreal quality. At the end of 1990 the downtown area had a vacancy rate of 22 percent in prime buildings, nearer 30 percent if secondary buildings were included. Rents were a measly nine to twelve dollars per square foot if the thirty-six-month rent-free periods given away with ten-year leases are taken into account. The error of the Japanese banks, and the Japanese owners whom they mostly financed, was to assume that the downtown area is the commercial center of Los Angeles as midtown Manhattan is to New York or Marunouchi is to Tokyo. In fact Los Angeles does not have a commercial center per se. The local Californian banks understood this and stayed out of the market, though they still have more than their fair share of dud property loans elsewhere in the state.

The Japanese banks' assets in America booked by these branches and agencies are considerable. They are in the $20 billion range or higher per bank, or the equivalent of a medium-sized regional bank in Japan. This is real money even by the standards of Japan's big city banks. Figures compiled by Schaefer and Associates, an accounting and consulting firm based in Claremont, California, show that the Industrial Bank of Japan is the largest Japanese bank in California, with assets of $8.1 billion in that state alone as of June 1991, down from an even larger $10.7 billion at the end of 1990. Second is Fuji Bank, with $5.4 billion in assets as of June 1991. In total the Japanese branches and agencies had $65 billion of assets booked in California alone in June 1991. These are chunky exposures given the questionable nature of some of the lending. One leading Los Angeles–based property consultant who has many of the Japanese banks for clients commented in early 1992 that he knew personally of about $3 billion to $4 billion of property in America financed by IBJ that was "under water." A banker at Long-Term Credit Bank, IBJ's rival, confirms the same scale of problem American loans facing his bank.

The foreign lending spree came to an abrupt halt during the second half of 1990. It was clear by this time that the collapse of the Tokyo stock market signaled more than a temporary correction. Until the end of 1991 the Japanese banks in America had one thing in their favor. America's famously stern bank regulators had refrained from rigorous examination of the loan portfolios of the Japanese banks' branches and agencies, for two reasons. First, being wholesale banks, they had no federally insured retail depositors to worry about. Second, many of the loans made were to Japanese entities and were backed in some way by Japanese shares and properties, which were thought to be safe collateral because of their sky-high valuations. However, the sharp declines in both those markets, as well as the increasingly visible financial problems of many of the Japanese companies that the Japanese banks financed in America, have now provoked regulators' interest. In the last three months of 1991 professional appraisers received a flurry of requests from Japanese banks for up-to-date valuations of the American properties they have financed in order to prepare for loan examinations by inspectors from the Office of the Comptroller of the Currency. The bankers will not like the answers they get back. The value of Los Angeles office buildings, for example, had by then fallen by up to one-third from late-1980s levels.

Loan exams can result in huge rises in the number of loans classified as nonperforming, as so many American banks have found to their chagrin in recent years. American banks have often been made to declare loans nonperforming even when the borrower is still paying interest because regulators have determined that the underlying collateral (usually property) has fallen in value by an amount that puts the borrower's ability to repay in doubt. So the risk for the Japanese banks, and indeed the likelihood given the rotten condition of their portfolios, is that the American regulators will make them increase loan-loss reserves against problem loans and use up precious capital just when it is urgently needed back home. This can only heighten the mounting concern within Japan about the deteriorating quality of the banks' domestic loan portfolios.

American banks, however, will welcome the regulators' interest in their Japanese competitors. They have become increasingly fed up with the attitudes of the Japanese banks when they are partners in a syndicate with a problem loan. Japanese banks will often refuse to foreclose on a property, using the lame excuse that they cannot take ownership of property without the permission of the finance ministry. They are also reluctant to get involved in proactive strategies, such as restructurings, to deal with problem loans, let alone more sophisticated techniques like securitization that are now favored by American banks. Rather, the Japanese banks' preferred approach has been to sit on their hands and literally do nothing. This has the merit of preventing them from having to admit to a loss, which would mean wiping out capital. Such prevarication, however, slows up the loan-recovery process to the detriment of all creditors, since property that stands empty in America (if not necessarily in Japan) tends to lose its value fast. This may well be another reason why American bank regulators decided to wade in.

Japanese problems are not solely derived from syndicated lending. They have also made some disastrous acquisitions overseas. Fuji Bank, for example, boasted about its aggressive entry into the American property and LBO market through its purchase of Heller, a Chicago-based financial-services subsidiary, in its 1989 annual report. This proved a classic example of bad timing. The Japanese banks also went beserk in Europe at the very end of the 1980s, sucked in predictably by then-fashionable 1992 Eurohysteria. They financed, for example, the final hurrah in London's commercial property boom. Japanese banks' loans for British property rose 56 percent in 1989 from £2.3 billion to £3.7 billion, or more than 10 percent of total property loans in Britain. The City of London, the financial center, is now glutted with vacant office space that serves as yet another tragicomic legacy of 1980s' financial fever.

The Japanese banks' mindless pursuit of asset growth in foreign markets they often knew little about is now over. They are either withdrawing altogether or at least trying to make sure they earn a better return. Their practical problem is that it is impossible to shrink quickly. It is hard to sell assets that yield almost nothing for the simple reason that no one wants to buy them. This leaves them little alternative but to run off credits as they come up for renewal.

The Japanese banks must now increase their loan margins both at home and abroad since they can no longer count on the Tokyo stock market to keep bailing them out by boosting their capital. This is a lesson that top management now understands but has only recently begun to act on, for there is a problem in such large organizations of communicating that message down to the branch level, where the pursuit of asset growth is an ingrained habit. Even now, city banks are reluctant to concede that expansion is a luxury they can no longer afford. Peer pressure from rivals in copycat Japan means that no bank wants to be the first to break ranks and start shrinking.

Still, with their traditional corporate customers long departed, Japanese banks have for some time been seeking to pursue more lucrative forms of lending at home. Consumer lending offers the most room for long-term expansion, because the Japanese still save a lot and have only in recent years begun to acquire a taste for borrowing. The Japanese banks have barely begun to tap the consumer market, though lending in this area has risen fast in recent years. Sanwa, for example, more than doubled its consumer lending (including mortgages) from 7 percent of total loans in 1986 to 15 percent in 1990; most city banks show similar patterns. The growth in this sort of lending will now slow in line with the slowing economy. But over the long term, there is lots of potential. Total lending to individuals (excluding mortgages) is only 3 percent of banks' total lending; mortgages make up another 11 percent of total lending. There also is lots of wealth to tap. At the end of September 1991, the personal sector's gross financial assets (excluding shares) totaled ¥777 trillion, or ¥19 million ($143,000) per household, a remarkable figure. This is arguably the Japanese economy's greatest strength and the main reasons why the purging of the excesses of the Bubble Economy, though extremely painful and a severe jolt to the nation's collective psychology, will not prove terminal.

The best hope for consumer lending is credit cards. Just how much potential this market offers is clear from a comparison with America, where credit cards have proved a gold mine for banks and have helped some to stave off disaster. For example, credit card income accounted for 90 percent of struggling Chase Manhattan's net income in 1990. So far, lots of plastic has been issued in Japan, but from the banks' point of view the results have been disappointing. The problem is that bank credit cards in Japan suffer from a key handicap. Consumers are not allowed to borrow against bank plastic, which means that outstanding balances have to be paid off monthly. The Ministry of International Trade and Industry (MITI), which regulates consumer finance, has now agreed to allow the introduction of revolving credit in 1992. Then Japanese banks can earn the 20 percent interest rates currently enjoyed by Japan's consumer-credit companies, which are allowed to extend credit on the plastic they issue.

Still, the rush into consumer lending has its own risks, as is becoming increasingly clear in countries like America and Britain. Even in traditionally conservative Japan the surge in consumer lending that did occur during the 1980s is now resulting in a surge in personal bankruptcies as the economy slows. Often, liberal use of credit cards is to blame. There were 166 million credit cards outstanding in 1990, up threefold from 1983. Gross consumer debt, excluding mortgages, totaled ¥67 trillion at the end of March 1991 (¥445,000 per household), up more than sevenfold from the 1989 total of ¥9 trillion.

But if consumer lending is the future in an increasingly con-sumerist Japan, where in the longer term people will spend more and save less, property-backed lending currently dominates banks' loan portfolios. During the property boom the average size of a bank mortgage has doubled from ¥5.6 million in 1984 to ¥11 million in 1990. The city banks have increased their share of the mortgage market from 13 percent to 22 percent during the same time. That share would be bigger were it not for the role played by the government-owned Housing Loan Corporation, which lends money for mortgages at rates significantly below those charged by banks. Home borrowers tend to use bank mortgages to top up when they need more than the maximum provided by government sub-sidy. Many employees also receive subsidized mortgages from their employers, further isolating them from the rigors of the market.

But mortgages are only one part of banks' property exposure. Nearly 75 percent of city banks' loans go to small businesses, and many of these loans are backed by property, often without being formally classified as such. The growth in financing of small companies during the second half of the 1980s is also clear from a surge in corporate overdrafts. Funds borrowed from approved overdraft facilities rose from 2 percent to 19 percent (or ¥41.6 trillion) of total outstanding loans between March 1981 and October 1991, according to Bank of Japan statistics. Overdrafts are the riskiest sort of lending since the bankers themselves have little idea about how their funds are being used.

Many other loans backed by property went through the conduit of Japan's nonbank banks. These are mainly leasing companies, consumer-finance companies, and mortgage companies, though there are many other sorts of nonbank lenders. All of them have one limiting feature in common. They cannot sell commercial paper to investors (as American finance companies can) and so are almost entirely dependent on bank credit for their funding. These secondary financial institutions have lent the banks' money on to more speculative property players prepared to pay higher interest rates for financing. Indeed, these loans were often deliberately used by the banks during the boom to circumvent official restrictions on lending to property companies and also to channel loans to risky or shady borrowers they preferred not to be seen lending to directly. The numbers are vast. Japanese banks had lent some ¥90 trillion to nonbanks and housing loan companies at the end of March 1991. Many of these loans have now gone bad and will end up on the banks' own balance sheets. A concerned Bank of Japan made it clear in the summer of 1991 that banks were expected to stand behind loans made by their nonbank affiliates to property companies. The central bank's aim was to reinforce Japan's so-called main-bank system under which the biggest lender in a bankruptcy assumes the debts of nearly all other creditors. Where a company is considered salvageable it will send a team of staff members into the troubled entity to manage the debt restructuring.

The problem for the authorities is that the condition of the loan portfolios of the 30,000-odd nonbanks remains something of a mystery, since they are mostly private companies that do not publish accounts. They were even more of a mystery before a concerned finance ministry, worried about the credit exposure of its bank charges, ordered a pioneering study to be carried out in 1990 in order to learn just what these fringe financial institutions had been up to in an effort both to gauge the scale of the credit risk to the banks' own balance sheets and to the financial system as a whole. Prior to this the nonbanks' lending activities went largely unregulated, a state of affairs that made America's savings and loans regulators look almost zealous by comparison. The finance ministry's troubleshooters were appalled at what they discovered. Too often, it seems, prudent career bankers became the wildest sort of speculators when they left a bank and moved to its nonbank affiliate.

The finance ministry's first study focused on the top two hundred nonbanks, which are reckoned to account for about 70 percent of nonbanks' total lending. It made scary reading. Between March 1989 and March 1990 these two hundred nonbanks increased the number of loans booked by 47 percent, compared with a 12 percent increase recorded by Japanese banks during the same period. Frantic loan growth went hand in hand with an increasing exposure to property. At the end of September 1990, 36 percent of outstanding nonbank loans had been made directly to property companies and 5 percent to construction companies. Another 14 percent of nonbank loans had gone to other nonbanks. Much of this money is thought to have ended up with property companies. Allowing for direct and indirect exposure, the finance ministry's startled bureaucrats calculated that about 60 percent of all nonbank loans had gone to the property and construction sectors. For banks, the equivalent figure is around 25 percent. If the exposures are large, the sums involved are enormous. As of March 1991, total lending by the three hundred biggest nonbanks was estimated by the finance ministry at ¥66 trillion, of which two-fifths was made directly to property and construction companies and two-thirds was collateralized by land. Total nonbank lending, including loans extended by housing-finance companies, was put at about ¥90 trillion, the equivalent of a third of the total lending of Japan's city banks, trust banks, and long-term credit banks. The nonbanks represent a significant part of banks' property exposure and a significant part of the banking system. Hence the Bank of Japan's timely warning.

Ironically, the nonbanks are also a worry for foreign banks based in Japan. The reason why again shows the degree to which Japan's credit system went berserk during the liquidity boom. Urged increasingly by a worried central bank to pull back from nonbank financing, Japanese banks in 1990 began actively encouraging foreign banks to step into the breach. They did so by agreeing (usually only verbally) to guarantee the loans the foreign banks extended. The ironic result was that after years of finding it hard to make loans at all in an essentially closed market, foreign banks went from feast to famine. Consequently, at the end of September 1990 foreign banks' loans to nonbanks totaled ¥6.3 trillion, or 58 percent of their total loans. The foreigners can now only hope that the Japanese banks honor their guarantees, and that their blind faith in the main-bank system will be vindicated.

There certainly can be no doubt that Japan's banks now face credit problems, at home and abroad, of enormous proportions. Bankruptcies in Japan totaled ¥8 trillion in 1991. Extrapolating from previous business downturns, Mikuni and Company calculates that bankruptcies will reach ¥10 trillion in each of the next three years. In addition, nearly fifty companies collectively owing around ¥20 trillion had by the end of 1991 admitted publicly to undergoing debt restructurings in a bid to stave off insolvency. There are numerous other companies that are staying afloat only by living off cash flow, by not paying interest on their debts, and by not writing checks. Bouncing a check is commercial suicide in Japan.

Despite this predicament, no Japanese bank at the end of 1991 had made any significant provisions against bad debts, an extraordinary fact. Consequently, their earnings and assets are significantly overstated. In collusion with compliant regulators, banks have decided to hang on in the hope they will eventually get their money back. This practice also has the merit for the regulators of containing the problem within the banking system for the moment. Banks also encourage debtors not to dump collateral, usually property, at depressed prices for fear of pulling down land values farther and thereby creating still more bad loans.

The Japanese banks' flexibility in dealing with bad debts needs to be contrasted with the dilemma facing American banks, because in this respect at least the playing fields are not equal. In America, nosy regulators can force banks to provide against questionable loans even when interest is still being paid. By contrast, banks in Japan enjoy almost limitless discretion. They are not required to disclose nonperforming loans at all. And they can report income from a troubled loan for a year after they have stopped receiving any interest from it. Astonishingly, no one in the finance ministry's banking bureau has the specific task of monitoring the adequacy of reserves against bad debts. Bankers say that whether approval is given to reserve against a problem loan depends on whom at the Ministry of Finance they happen to talk to. This peculiar state of affairs arises because Japanese regulation of problem loans works in the opposite way one would expect. Instead of the finance ministry enforcing prudential standards, it is up to the banks to ask the regulators for permission to reserve on a case by case basis. This reflects the attitude of the tax authorities. The banks are the biggest taxpayers in Japan, and loan reserves can be deducted against tax only if permission is specifically granted. Traditionally, the tax man has only allowed deductions for reserves against truly bad credits, where the borrower is bankrupt or as good as.

This regulatory attitude may have its origins in tax issues, but in the present context of mounting bad debts it has provided a convenient excuse for banks to avoid owning up to their problems. Such flexibility allowed the banks, in their financial year ended March 31, 1991, to reduce the new reserves they set aside against bad debts even though their nonperforming loans were by then already clearly rising. The point of this ruse was to prop up earnings that had been badly dented by the stock market crash. The ability to avoid declaring a loan nonperforming until after a full year of nonpayment of interest also means that banks are unlikely to start really owning up to the true condition of their loan portfolios until they report their results for the financial year ending March 1993. To help them pull off this conjuring trick, banks have been trying to get borrowers who are not paying interest to come up with just 30 percent of what is owed during the financial year. This enables them to pretend that all interest has been paid, or at least to lend the borrower still more money with which to pay the interest.

Such tricks aside, Japanese financial institutions, banks and nonbanks, have lent far too much to finance property development, and this exposure does not just include lending directly to property and construction companies. Many companies that were not property specialists also became active in property development during the bubble years, attracted by the lure of soaring prices. In addition, many normal business loans are also backed by property, since this is traditionally banks' collateral of choice. So in one form or another, property supports a huge chunk, perhaps as much as 80 percent, of Japanese banks' total loans of some ¥450 trillion, against which they had reserved a mere ¥3 trillion at the end of September 1991. This is an extraordinarily risky strategy for anyone who accepts the conventional maxim of prudent banking outside Japan, namely that loans gone bad should be owned up to, provided for, and reserved against. True, the year ending March 31, 1990, marked the final spike when city banks' outstanding loans backed by property soared by 22 percent. Since then growth in bank property lending has been flat to negative as the central bank has finally imposed its wishes on the marketplace, though the flow of credit to the property sector continued for several more crazy months through the foreign banks and Japanese nonbanks.

The Bank of Japan's attitude has been clear. Governor Mieno may have liked to say that rising land prices fuel inflation. But his real concern has been less with the consumer price index than with puncturing the speculative bubble before it burst of its own accord more violently and from an even more extreme level of overvaluation, unleashing even more damage on the banking system.

The Bank of Japan was right to be concerned, and Mieno

deserves every credit for seizing the initiative by raising interest rates as soon as he took office at the end of 1989, despite the misgivings of many inside the finance ministry. In 1990 an evidently concerned Bank of Japan sent teams to Britain and America to study the examples of London's secondary banking crisis in 1974 and America's more recent $500 billion savings and loan disaster. Both financial debacles had their origins partly in interest rate deregulation and both culminated in lots of bad property debts. But in 1990, the Bank of Japan remained confident that it was in full control, that it could become the first central bank in history to puncture a speculative bubble of such monumental proportions without damaging the real economy.

The central bank was not quite so smugly self-assured by September 1991 when it published a report with the dry title "Credit Risk Management of Financial Institutions Related to Lending." The booklet may have been written in bland technical prose, but its contents provided clear evidence of the Bank of Japan's growing alarm at the evident deterioration of credit standards during the late 1980s. The booklet reflects the naïveté of the official bureaucratic mind, which assumes that rules will be adhered to in the midst of a credit boom, when history indicates precisely the opposite, and it echoes the resulting shock when the bureaucrats discover the extent to which lending standards have lapsed. The report notes that financial institutions' credit departments became "dominated" by those seeking to promote loans; that loans were made against land and shares that were "over-optimistically valued"; and that in some cases there was no on-site inspection of a property before a loan was made against it.

The central bank's recommendations are laudably sensible but hopelessly belated. Financial institutions are admonished "to comprehend in detail the size of their problem loans and non-performing assets" and "to increase loan-loss reserves against non-performing assets." Yet this is precisely what the banks are *not* doing, because in large part the regulatory system actively discourages these actions. Instead, banks adopt a strategy of hanging on with fingers crossed. This is to court disaster.

What worries the Bank of Japan is that the government (or rather the taxpayers) will one day be obliged to start bailing out banks and depositors, just as now happens with depressing regularity in America. Mieno wants desperately to avoid this development. Japan has a deposit insurance scheme like America's, but hardly anyone knows it exists, for the very good reason that no bank has gone bust since 1942. Deposits are insured up to ¥10 million, and the insurance fund, which was set up in 1971, has capital of only ¥455 million plus the ability to borrow from the central bank ¥500 billion. This may not be enough in the coming crisis. A study by McKinsey's Tokyo office in mid-1991 concluded that thirty banks, with total assets of ¥2.6 trillion, were in danger of failing. (This is a far too optimistic estimate; a firm like McKinsey naturally does not want to appear alarmist.) The first chink in the armor appeared in July 1991 when it was announced that money from the deposit insurance fund would be tapped for the first time ever to help pay for the forced purchase of Toho Sogo Bank, a small local bank with bad debts of ¥20 billion, by Iyo Bank, a medium-size regional bank. Japan's fine record of no bank failures in its postwar history* is now threatened, with all that means for depositors' confidence.

The mammoth city banks were not the only financial institutions to catch the property bug. In October 1991, *Kinyu Business*, a respected monthly business magazine, looked at banks' exposure to companies that had either gone bust or had been forced to reschedule their debts. By this publication's reckoning, the city banks fared comparatively well. Their problem loans were estimated at ¥2.8 trillion, which was the equivalent of only twice their reported profits and 13 percent of their hidden assets, or the

---

*It should not be assumed that Japanese banks were always safe. Like America in the 1930s, Japan suffered from its own financial panics and bank failures earlier this century. In 1927 Japan suffered a full-scale banking panic with the collapse of the Suzuki *zaibatsu* and its satellite, the Bank of Kobe. (The *zaibatsu* were broken up by the Americans during the post-1945 occupation only to reemerge as the less rigidly structured though still interconnected *keiretsu*.)

unrealized gains on the shares they own. Given the lack of adequate provisions against nonperforming loans in Japanese accounting practice, it is these unrealized share gains that function as Japanese banks' loan-loss reserves. The Japanese trust banks, which in theory specialize in trust business but in reality are heavily involved in property, were in much grimmer shape. By June 1990 they had lent 52 percent of their total loans of ¥53.9 trillion to property-backed credits; 36 percent of their total loans went to nonbanks. *Kinyu Business* put the trust banks' problem loans at ¥2 trillion, or eight times their previous year's operating profits and 31 percent of their hidden assets. Trust banks suffer from an important constraint. They cannot transfer bad loans to related subsidiary companies if the loans are from their trust accounts (which is where most of their property loans are). The trust bank is not the legal owner of these loans and is therefore legally constrained from selling them. Such transfers are a standard city bank ruse to conceal bad credits, even though a bad credit remains the responsibility of the parent bank, wherever it might be held.

A symbol of the trust banks' problems is Juso, a company that the seven major trust banks originally set up with capital of ¥800 billion to provide housing loans to individuals. In the late 1980s Juso changed direction and lent heavily to property companies. By October 1991 it had amassed ¥2 trillion of debt and was demanding that its trust bank owners reduce its interest payments and forgive some of its debt. Since the trust banks' joint investment in the firm is equal to 23 percent of their total capital, Juso has a great deal of leverage in negotiations, since more than its own survival is at stake.

The trust banks' woes are repeated at the three long-term credit banks, the traditional lenders to Japanese industry in the 1950s and early 1960s, when credit was rationed by MITI. As of June 1990, 47 percent of their total loans of ¥43.9 trillion were backed by property. By October 1991 the dire consequences of that exposure were becoming clear. The three long-term credit banks had problem loans of ¥2.4 trillion, which was equivalent to eleven times their operating profits and 38 percent of their hidden assets, according to *Kinyu Business.* Worst hit according to the magazine was the smallest, Nippon Credit Bank. It had ¥937 billion of these problem loans, equaling nearly 90 percent of its hidden assets. (Nippon Credit Bank disputes this figure.) Long-Term Credit Bank (LTBC) had ¥857 billion and IBJ had ¥625 billion of the loans according to *Kinyu Business.*

These figures represent the exposures of Japan's major banks. The regional banks are also vulnerable because they do not have the same level of hidden assets to cover bad debts. There are, for example, at least twenty major regional banks where it only requires 3 percent of total loans to go bad before the bank will have used up all of its loan-loss reserves and unrealized share gains and will have to start drawing on shareholders' capital.

But what perhaps worried the regulators the most, at least in the early days of the bubble's bursting, were Japan's smaller regional financial institutions. There are 926 secondary regional banks (formerly known as *sogo* banks), and *shinkin* banks, the local equivalent of America's credit unions. These small institutions also found themselves chasing higher-yielding assets as the cost of their deposits rose. As with America's thrifts, one natural response for such local banks was to lend to local property developers. This is why many remoter rural areas of Japan were caught up in the land bubble even though they did not have the underlying economic activity to justify astronomical prices. The small local banks also became aggressive investors in the stock market since this seemed the easiest way to raise the yield on their assets and so fund more costly deposits. These pressures explain why the central bank has in recent years been dispatching staff to help prop up financial institutions all over the country and why the local press has been instructed to keep quiet about the problems of small banks. They also explain why the Bank of Japan wants to force weak *shinkin* banks into stronger hands through forced mergers before depositor confidence is shaken by a wave of failures. The central bank is right to be worried; in some rural areas there is only one bank serving the community. Unfortunately, there are now too many problems for officials to keep on top of, and the stronger banks are increasingly reluctant to weaken themselves financially by taking over bust institutions. In a deregulated world the larger banks are less willing to do what central bank or finance ministry officials tell them, especially when it means using up precious capital.

Consolidation of the Japanese banking industry is both a desirable and expected consequence of deregulation. The tricky part is getting from here to there. Since 1945 the Japanese system has been successful in getting strong banks to take over failing banks, as in 1986 when Sumitomo Bank bought Heiwa Sogo Bank, a Tokyo-based regional. The trouble is that now, thanks to BIS pressures and a depressed stock market, there are fewer banks financially capable of mounting such rescues, even assuming they would want to. The Japanese government will increasingly have to guarantee such bailouts, just as it tapped deposit insurance funds to help finance the rescue of Toho Sogo Bank by Iyo Bank. Just how much government money will be spent sorting out this mess will depend on how far land prices fall.

# 3

# Land

For all its high-tech gadgetry and automated vending machines, Japan remains a feudal society at heart whose members, like peasants throughout the ages, believe in the value of land. Behind many a salaryman there is a grandfather or elderly relative still toiling in the fields. Their blue-suited salaried offspring still count their net worth primarily as the dirt on which their prefabricated houses sit.*

This cultural fact makes it hard to discuss the issue of land prices in Japan in purely economic terms. For status in Japan, as in all feudal systems, rests on the possession of land. This explains why the myth that property only goes up in price, regardless of business cycles, has been perpetuated with greater emotional conviction in Japan than in America or Europe. This myth is one powerful reason why Japanese property reached a level of overvaluation that makes it worthy for inclusion in any updated version of Charles Mackay's classic nineteenth-century history of speculative manias, *Extraordinary Popular Delusions and the Madness of Crowds.*

The bald facts of Japan's land bubble are certainly worthy of

---

*In Japan virtually all of the value of a property lies in the land, not the building. As a result, buildings are knocked down and replaced with almost reckless abandon.

comparison with the seventeenth century's tulip mania in Holland. America is twenty-five times bigger than Japan in terms of its physical area. Yet Japan's property market at the end of 1989 was still reckoned by sober people in the government's Management and Coordination Agency to be worth over ¥2,000 trillion, or four times the estimated ¥500 trillion value of American property. This is truly history's greatest accumulation of wealth in one country. It creates some ludicrous anomalies. In early 1990 Japan in theory was able to buy the whole of America by selling off metropolitan Tokyo, or all of Canada by hawking the grounds of the Imperial Palace.

Japan's most recent land boom, which began in 1985 and only ended in 1990 when the flow of credit to the property sector was at last curtailed, has hugely boosted many individuals' wealth, since 62 percent of Japanese households own the home in which they live. There are said to be 1 million people living within a thirty-six-mile radius of central Tokyo owning property worth more than ¥500 million; there are another 3.5 million people owning property worth ¥100 million. Yet there is a widespread notion among both Japanese and foreigners that such figures are merely statistical artifacts and are essentially meaningless because land in Japan hardly ever changes hands. This is to miss the point entirely. Land values do not just represent theoretical wealth. A link between theory and reality is provided by Japan's credit system. In fact, Japanese banks have a long tradition of lending against the value of an asset, unlike Western banks, which lend against the rental income that can be earned from a property. Given the shared values of Japanese society, there is no better collateral than a deed proving ownership of land. Land can be easily turned into instant credit, as it was in huge quantities during the years of the Bubble Economy. It would not be an exaggeration to say that Japan operates on a land standard, just as the major economic powers at the beginning of this century fixed their currencies to gold.

As we have already seen, the exposure of Japanese financial institutions to property is enormous. Any precipitous decline in land values would threaten the balance sheets of Japan's lending

circle. It has gone from being an illiquid market where no one wants to sell (the traditional condition in this land-worshiping society) to an equally illiquid market where no one wants to buy. A sum of ¥50 trillion is huge. Such pent-up supply in such an illiquid market can only mean one thing: an eventual steep fall in prices. That the finance ministry did not feel able to lift the credit controls before the beginning of 1992 because the National Land Agency figures still showed a national rise in land prices reflects the bureaucratic mind-set. It shows a misplaced faith in administrators' ability to fine-tune the impact of their policies and a failure to understand the dynamics of the ebb and flow of credit in a deregulated economy. The result was simply to keep the market frozen for a few more months, thereby guaranteeing that buyers and sellers would grow even farther apart. By late 1991 genuine bids for office buildings in the key Tokyo and Osaka metropolitan markets were already 30 to 50 percent below "official" National Land Agency prices. Thirty percent of ¥2,000 trillion is a lot of wealth to replace if prices are suddenly reduced to market levels.

Officialdom's complacency was dangerous. It underestimated the extent to which liquidity-driven markets can fluctuate, especially when credit is cut off abruptly. Mieno, the Bank of Japan's governor, has stated in public that he would be happy to see an orderly 20 percent decline in land prices. The crash thus far may have been silent, because of the lack of transactions, but it will end up being far more than 20 percent and ultimately not so orderly. Everyone knew that the end of credit controls would trigger a return of some liquidity to the market as creditworthy buyers would once again be able to obtain financing. But the effect of this influx would, perversely, be bearish. Since the would-be sellers so far outnumbered the would-be buyers, the real issue was how far prices would have to decline to allow the market to clear. One point was apparent: the declines were likely to be of a magnitude that would trigger a whole new wave of bankruptcies. The distress behind the scenes will become increasingly visible once the credit controls are lifted and the bad debts grow and the banks are forced finally to own up to them. This process will be a painfully drawn-out affair since property is not like the stock market, where the prices of shares can be checked daily in the newspaper. The real test of the market will only come when the full magnitude of the fall in values dawns on the landowning public. Then it will be interesting to see if the wealth effect takes hold and there is a consequent depressing effect on consumer spending. Consumption accounts for 57 percent of Japan's gross national product. Falls in housing prices have certainly helped depress consumer sentiment in countries like America, Britain, and Australia in recent years as ordinary folk see the value of the main asset on their personal balance sheet decline. It is astonishing that most mainstream economists in Tokyo still see no risk of a similar development in Japan despite the fact that land is most families' main asset. The complacent argument they peddle is that householders will not notice the drop in values because there are so few transactions. This seems farfetched. Even today, most Japanese consumers remain notoriously cautious, partly because of the traumatic legacy of war and partly because of the lack of pension provision for their old age. If Mrs. Watanabe hears that a piece of land in her community has sold for 40 percent less than it was reckoned to be worth eighteen months earlier, she will surely feel significantly poorer and will adjust her spending accordingly, regardless of whether she has taken on debt against the property or not. And many people have taken on lots of debt.

An illustration of the way Japanese people use land as the most convenient form of instant credit is provided by the Japanese prime minister, Kiichi Miyazawa. Before he moved into the prime minister's official residence next to the Japanese Diet (parliament) in late 1991, he lived in Tokyo's fashionable Harajuku district. There are two curious features about his house. First, it does not belong to Miyazawa. Rather, the land registry shows the property is owned by Hiroko Kanbara, a female member of the Kanbara family, which is active in shipbuilding and a bulwark of the local business community in Miyazawa's home town of Fukuyama in Hiroshima prefecture. Miyazawa pays a nominal (for Tokyo) monthly rent of ¥100,000 for this generous gift from his political patrons, according to mandatory disclosure figures released by the Japanese government. Second, the title deed shows the property has been used by various Kanbara family corporate entities as collateral to borrow, as of June 1989, ¥13.2 billion from seven banks. This is a lot of debt, even by Japanese standards. The 0.15-acre site is worth only about ¥2.7 billion, based on its estimated market value in early 1991 of ¥15 million per *tsubo* (3.3 square meters and the standard Japanese property measure), or less than one-quarter of the debt it supports. Most of the money was borrowed in the late 1980s when shipbuilding was going through a lean spell and banks were desperate to make property loans. During that period borrowers like the Kanbara family kept increasing their loans as the value of their collateral soared, often capitalizing any interest they owed in the process.

If banks are worried about the value of their collateral eroding, politicians also fret because most of their own wealth is tied up in land, as is clear from the mandatory disclosure figures. Miyazawa, for example, disclosed assets (including those held in the name of direct family members) that total ¥1.7 billion. Three plots of land account for most of this total, securities and deposits for just ¥49 million. Most other cabinet members are similarly placed, with land accounting for nearly all their declared wealth. It is no wonder that no one in Japan's establishment dares admit to the possibility of a land crash. They, like the banks, are locked into this sort of asset in what has good claim to be the world's most illiquid market.

The first signs of a public debate in Japan about whether property prices could fall finally appeared several months after stock prices started sliding. In October 1990 NHK, Japan's public television broadcasting system, showed a series of five programs complete with live phone-ins and opinion polls on how a dramatic fall in land prices could hurt the Japanese economy and the banking system. Hypothetical numbers abounded. One scary figure provided by a research institute backed by Mitsubishi Bank was that a 50 percent decline in land values over four years could trigger ¥10 trillion of bad debts. This now looks like a very conservative estimate. A year later, Salomon Brothers published research that forecast that, in the worst of two postulated outcomes, bad debts could reach ¥20 trillion. As with America's savings and loan crisis, the final tally will keep rising because of the immense scale of the problem and because banks and officials are still trying to pretend that the problem does not exist. Because virtually every loan in the banking system is collateralized by land in some form or other, bad debts could reach ¥100 trillion and still be less than 25 percent of total loans. This may sound alarmist. It is not.

More anecdotal evidence of creeping doubts about the supposed invulnerability of land as a store of value was provided by the response of Fuji Bank's research institute to an article published in *The Economist* in August 1990 on why Japanese property prices would fall sharply. The bank asked the author to reply to a series of prepared questions, seeking further information on why *The Economist* thought land prices would drop. The incident showed that Fuji's senior management had begun to have doubts about the size of their property loan portfolio, which was perhaps not so surprising since the bank's property-backed loans rose by 30 percent in the year ending March 1990. But, more interestingly, it transpired that opinion in the bank's own research institute was at that point divided fifty-fifty on whether, as the bankers put it, the "land myth" would prevail. This reflected an unusual, and therefore troubling, level of uncertainty. A year before no one would have doubted that the myth would indeed prevail. A year later most informed people would have agreed it would not. By then the only issue was how manageable the decline would be.

By the end of 1991 those companies most heavily exposed to property were at or past the point of capitulation; the only issue was whether they owed enough money, say over ¥100 billion each, that the banks would have to support them because they could not afford not to. Banks had long conceded, albeit tacitly, that the plunge into property lending had been ill conceived. They were now battening down the hatches and hoping they could hang on throughout the downturn, whether it lasts three years or five, without having to resort to dumping collateral on a depressed market. Signs of weakness abounded. One was the plunge in the number of condominiums sold within the first month of being put on the market. The sales rate was still in the low 90 percent range at the beginning of 1990. By mid-1991 it was under 50 percent in Tokyo and under 25 percent in Osaka. The Osaka region was the last to peak, having seen explosive price rises as late as 1989; its bust has therefore been correspondingly both faster and more severe. The first question businessmen now ask one another in that commercially minded city is "Are you paying interest?"

In November 1991 the *Nihon Keizai Shimbun,* Japan's leading business daily, began to let out some of the bad news. It publicized the results of one of its regular surveys, which confirmed that office rents in new buildings were down by as much as 20 percent in central Tokyo. This contradicted the widely held belief that rents cannot fall in Tokyo because of the sheer pressure on space. The same month a Ministry of Construction survey of existing-home sales reported a sharp drop in the price of houses and apartments in the year ending October 1991. Existing detached houses in the twenty-three wards of metropolitan Tokyo had lost 37 percent of their value, while in suburban Saitama outside Tokyo plots of building land had declined in price by 41 percent. These are stunning falls for a market that provided collateral for the world's biggest borrowing binge. Yet the 62 percent of Japanese households that own their homes were still not yet fully alert to the extent to which prices had fallen, mainly because continuing credit controls had so reduced the number of transactions.

Most property developers' natural response to this spreading weakness has been to hang on in the desperate hope that prices would recover and bail them out. They are desperate because history shows that credit booms of this degree of excess do not unwind quickly, especially when would-be sellers refuse to take a loss. Many of the few sales concluded were cozy inside deals at National Land Agency "official" prices and therefore were at least 30 percent above market price. A good example of this was the Long-Term Credit Bank's (LTCB) sale in August 1991 of its headquarters building in Tokyo's Otemachi financial district to Nippon Landic, the bank's property-development arm. Analysts estimate that the wretched property affiliate paid nearly ¥100 million per *tsubo* for the site, or roughly the official price. LTCB itself appears to have profited handsomely; the property was valued at cost in its accounts at ¥2 billion but was sold for ¥100 billion.

The bank used that capital gain for tax purposes to set against loan losses it had sustained that year. It had some well-known credit problems to shoulder. LTCB is, for example, the main bank to EIE, the maverick property-development company to which it has lent some $1 billion, or about one-sixth of EIE's total borrowings of $6 billion. EIE is noteworthy because it embarked on one of the most extraordinary of all the Japanese overseas shopping binges during the Bubble Economy. The company bought everything from the usual Los Angeles, New York, and London hotels and office buildings (it owns the Regent Beverly Wilshire in Los Angeles and is building another Regent hotel on Manhattan's Fifty-seventh Street, which has been billed as New York's most expensive hotel) to more exotic items like floating hotels in Saigon. Barely known inside Japan, EIE's chairman, Harunori Takahashi, was beloved by foreign correspondents in Tokyo because of his unorthodox flamboyant approach. He was featured in numerous articles in the foreign press while he was still flying high. A far cry from the dull blue-suited salaryman, Takahashi had been expelled from a smart Tokyo private school and had a father-in-law who had been one of Japan's largest stock market speculators before (according to Takahashi) being wiped out when the likes of Nomura ganged up against him. Takahashi's business philosophy was "to keep it simple." This was no understatement. His empire was based solely on his ability to persuade the banks to keep lending. When LTCB finally called a halt and took control of EIE and the extent of the bank's exposure became known, officials at the finance ministry privately expressed astonishment and dismay that this respectable bank could have lent so much to such a dubious concern. The aim of the LTCB-led restructuring now under way is to try to sell ¥250 billion of EIE's stated assets of ¥690 billion. A team of twenty-five LTCB executives is inside EIE running the company. Their role is described on their business cards as "EIE: Special Project."

The key consideration for LTCB when it sold its headquarters building to its property affiliate was tax planning. A change in the tax laws that took effect at the start of 1992 means that companies not directly in the property business (like banks) can no longer offset gains from the sales of property against losses (like bad loans to EIE) sustained in their core banking businesses. So Nippon Landic came in very useful to LTCB. However, if LTCB could have sold to a genuine outsider at the same fancy price, without having to stuff its affiliate in this rather questionable manner, it would presumably have done so. But the buyers were not around. The decline in the property market was by then too far advanced.

Japan could not expect an army of foreign investors to come to the rescue of their property market in the way that gung-ho Japanese investors (like EIE) had helped many American owners unload their property holdings at the top of the market in the late 1980s. The prices in Japan were, in relative terms, still far too high. In addition, the consequences of the foray into overseas property were mostly disastrous for Japanese buyers. By the end of 1991, with their own property market imploding, Japanese property players were busy trying to sell overseas trophy properties, bought only a few years previously as "long-term investments," in an increasingly desperate bid to cut their losses and raise some cash. Thus, cash-strapped Dai-Ichi Real Estate put New York's Tiffany Building up for sale just five years after buying it in 1986 for a record price (for Manhattan) of $959 per square foot. The hoped-for sale is part of a Mitsui Trust–led restructuring of Dai-Ichi Real Estate, under which the company is supposed to unload ¥120 billion of properties over three years. Almost all Dai-Ichi's overseas properties are up for sale.

Japanese investment in American property rose from $1.9 billion in 1985 to $16.5 billion in 1988 and $14.8 billion in 1989, according to figures compiled by Kenneth Leventhal and Company, a Los Angeles–based accounting firm specializing in real estate consulting. In 1991 Japanese investment slumped to $5.1 billion. In the beginning Japanese investors bought typical landmark "trophy" buildings in cities like New York and Los Angeles. They subsequently broadened their range, diversifying away from office buildings into hotel and resort projects, residential developments, and even raw land. The three favored areas for investment were California, Hawaii, and Guam, an American territory only three hours by plane from Japan. As they grew more comfortable and confident about investing overseas the Japanese ventured into fringe properties such as golf courses. Here they were following the prevailing trend at home.

Property companies piled into golf course development during the latter stages of the Bubble Economy in one of the final hurrahs of the property boom. More than 160 golf courses were built in Japan between 1989 and 1991. Another 1,200 are either under construction or have received planning approval. Many of them will probably never be completed because their developers will go bust or because concerned banks will pull in their loans. The economic rationale of many of these golf course developments hinged on preselling golf club memberships, the secondary trading of which constitutes an active market in Japan. Not surprisingly, given the national obsession with golf, this became a ludicrously overheated market in the late 1980s. An estimated 1.8 million people own golf club memberships in Japan; the prices of these memberships, which are traded like securities, range from a few million yen up to the ¥250 million range. At the peak, Japan's 1,700 golf courses were estimated to have a total membership market value of some $200 billion. This madness led predictably to fraudulent scams, which were only exposed when the business turned sour and prices dropped. As is to be expected wherever there is the lure of fast money, some of this fraudulent activity rubbed off on fund-seeking politicians. Thus in the summer of 1991 police raided the offices of the Ibaraki Country Club, north of Tokyo, which had sold 49,000 memberships instead of the 2,800 originally promised to enrolling members. In September of that year Shintaro Ishihara, Liberal Democratic Party member and the well-known coauthor (with Sony chairman Akio Morita) of the controversial Japanese best-seller *The Japan That Can Say No*, was accused of accepting ¥30 million in illegal political contributions from the operator of the Ibaraki golf club, Ken Mizuno. (In early 1992 Mizuno was prosecuted for evading ¥5.74 billion in taxes and ordered to pay ¥7.8 billion, including penalties.) In another scam the comically named Gatsby Golf Club was found by the Tokyo district court to have issued 30,000 memberships after promising to limit its members to 1,800. These sorts of excesses are now over, not least because the Nikkei Golf Club Membership Index had by the end of 1991 fallen by nearly 50 percent from its peak as available credit dried up and speculators realized that there is a physical limit to the number of golf courses even golf-mad Japan can accommodate and a financial limit to how much aspiring members are prepared to pay.

The Japanese certainly reflected their love of golf in the way they spent their money in America. Golf courses became a favorite target, especially since it was reasoned that Japanese tourists could be funneled through them in large numbers. The peak of the frenzy was the September 1990 $831 million purchase of California's Pebble Beach resort, one of America's most famous, by Cosmo World, a medium-size property company. Pebble Beach includes several golf courses and two luxury hotels. This acquisition provoked great controversy in America when it became known that the upstart Cosmo World planned to turn Pebble Beach into a private club and finance the project Japanese style by preselling memberships. The storm of protest was such that Mitsubishi Trust, the original financier, abruptly withdrew from the project. It already had enough problems on its plate with property loans going bad without this sort of unwanted high-profile exposure. Cosmo World was bailed out temporarily by Itoman, the medium-size Osaka trading company that was on the verge of becoming embroiled in its own scandal back in Japan. It bought ¥85 billion worth of golf club memberships from Cosmo World at top of the market prices; Cosmo World used these proceeds to pay off Mitsubishi Trust. This act of seeming charity was explained by the close relationship between Yoshihiko Kawamura, the former Itoman president (and central figure in the securities scandal, of which more later), and Minoru Isutani, chairman of Cosmo World. The purchase of the golf club memberships was commercial suicide for the already hugely indebted Itoman. As for Cosmo World, Kawamura's helping hand only temporarily staved off looming financial distress. In early 1992 Cosmo agreed to sell Pebble Beach for $500 million, or $341 million less than it paid for it. The buyer was a joint venture between Taiheiyo Club Incorporated, an established owner and operator of many Japanese golf courses, and Sumitomo Card Services, Japan's leading issuer of Visa cards. Sumitomo was involved because it had the misfortune to be Itoman's main bank.

Pebble Beach was only the most conspicuous example of extensive Japanese purchases of American golf courses. In a 1991 special report on Japanese golf course development in America, Arizona-based Mead Ventures estimated that, by market value, Japanese-owned golf courses in America accounted for as much as 5 percent of the total market value of all courses in America, though the Japanese probably owned at most 2 percent of the actual physical number of courses. The Japanese presence is most visible in Hawaii, where the Japanese own nearly all the private courses and are also building as many new courses. The Mead report predicts bravely that the number of Japanese-owned golf courses in Hawaii could double to more than eighty within five years. This is an absurdly optimistic forecast, a classic example of extrapolating past trends into the future. It takes no account of the bursting of the bubble and the resulting rationing of credit within Japan. The plain fact is that financing for many of these ventures is no longer available, nor in many cases is the collateral backing. Hawaii's resort property market has since collapsed along with California's property market, the other favored target of Japanese capital. Both overseas buying sprees have proved unmitigated disasters by most conventional measures.

Indeed, some of the most insane Japanese investments of the bubble years are to be found in Hawaii. Here Japanese developers bought or built resort hotels, financed by Japanese banks, without any consideration of the income that could be earned from these properties. Anthony Downs, a Brookings fellow, argues in a paper published by Salomon Brothers that this strategy hinged on the greater fool theory. Properties were designed to be sold on to "irrational" Japanese investors, since developers knew they could not possibly make money operating them. But if those "irrational" buyers ever existed they have long since disappeared with the crashes of Japan's stock and property markets.

Japanese investors bought or partly financed all but two of Hawaii's main resort hotels between early 1985 and early 1991. The most extravagant of these projects is the Grand Hyatt Wailea Resort and Spa on Maui, which has been billed as the most luxurious hotel ever built. The hotel sports, for example, a two-thousand-foot network of pools, grottoes, and rapids plus a "water elevator" that "raises and lowers swimmers using a system of canal-like locks," according to Hawaii's *Hospitality* magazine. The hotel, which opened in September 1991, cost some $600 million to build—more than $760,000 per room. Based on standard hotel economics, Downs reckons that it needs to charge $700 per room per night and achieve a 75 percent occupancy rate to break even. He concludes that since this is impossible in any tourist hotel on earth, the owners face a huge loss. One point is certain. The sheer opulence of this hotel will lure tourists away from other Japanese-owned hotels in Hawaii, making it harder for them to fill their rooms. Downs argues that many Japanese investors and small developers "will probably be ruined financially by their Hawaiian losses."

The developer of this Grand Hyatt and the owner of a 50 percent equity stake is TSA International, named after the company's president, Takeshi Sekiguchi. Sekiguchi is also the front man in several other high-profile, Japanese-financed luxury projects in Hawaii and California, most of them, including the Grand Hyatt, financed by the Industrial Bank of Japan. TSA's brochure lists fourteen such projects, most of them in Hawaii and the bulk of them described as "world class hotels." IBJ, for example, financed the Ko Olina development on Oahu in which TSA has a 60 percent stake. This is a case of a project that has been put on ice indefinitely by the bankers because of Hawaii's glut of luxury resorts. The original plan was to build 8 hotels and 5,000 luxury condominiums, which were supposed to sell for $5 million to $10 million each. None have been built so far, though four coves have been carved out of the shoreline and some roads have been constructed, and none may ever be, since the financing is no longer available. Originally IBJ had said it would guarantee to buy the condominiums because it thought it could sell them off to its major corporate clients as perks for chief executives. Now the bank does not want to commit another yen to the project.

Many American golf course developments, resort complexes, and other "luxury" properties will end up owned by Japanese banks, sold at fire sale prices, or abandoned uncompleted. When financing Japanese entities overseas Japanese banks are more inclined to take their money and run at the first hint of trouble, if they can afford to take the hit, than they are at home where they know the local market and are prepared to be far more patient. Within Japan they are also under strict social constraints. They do not want to be accused of upsetting the property market by dumping collateral. But overseas, if they can exit a loan and get 60 to 70 percent of their money back in lieu of the foreign collateral they lent against, Japanese banks will be strongly tempted to do so, especially if they can find a legitimate Japanese buyer to take the property off their hands, as happened with Pebble Beach. They can do this because in the Japanese system the debtor has almost no say during a restructuring or loan workout. This attitude does not apply to bigger debtors since there is too much money at stake, which banks dare not lose. In these cases recovery of the banks' money will demand years of patience and, as in the case of LTCB's management of EIE, a substantial investment of manpower. Often the bankers who made the loans in the first place are sent back to run the workout. In America such an overbearing attitude toward the debtor would probably trigger lawsuits. Should the Japanese banks ever decide to dump overseas assets en masse, in stark contrast to their restrained attitude thus far at home, it would certainly make those property markets where they have been active that much worse. This option cannot be ruled out, especially as the

Japanese banks tend to move together like sheep. The Japanese would then be exporting their bad-loan problems, which is a troubling thought, though one American trade negotiators have yet to address.

There are disasters aplenty from Japanese companies' forays into overseas property, but they are minor compared to the problems at home, where the amounts of money involved are so much greater because property values were bid up so much higher. As in many of the world's top city centers the speculation of recent years has resulted in a large increase in office space. Even in crowded Japan supply factors are not quite the prop to values they are usually thought to be. The amount of space under construction in Tokyo, Osaka, and Nagoya, the three major cities, has doubled since 1984. In 1990 alone, Tokyo developers began to build office space equal to almost 11 percent of the existing stock of buildings in the capital city. Mori Building, a major development company that has read the property cycle better than most, estimates that between 1990 and 1995 the Tokyo market will have to absorb an annual supply of 17.4 million square feet of floor space in new large office buildings. This is almost twice the 9.3-million-square-foot supply built annually in the previous five-year period. As a result, office rents for existing space in Tokyo are now almost stationary for the first time in recent memory. If rents actually start falling across the board, as they have already begun to do in new and secondary buildings, the myth about the invulnerability of prices in Japan's property market will be shattered. Another myth is that vacancy rates are microscopic. The figure usually quoted is the 0.25 percent published by the Japan Building Association, whose venerable membership includes only the five hundred largest owners of Tokyo's prime sites. James Capel's property analysts estimate that the real vacancy rate in the twenty-three wards of central Tokyo is more like 5 percent. The vacancy rate for recently completed buildings is double that and more, which is the main reason rents are now falling in those buildings.

This deteriorating picture has already frightened many in the property business, who have firsthand knowledge of market conditions. But most pundits, Japanese and foreign, have tended to view an orderly 20 percent decline in land values as the most likely outcome of the burst bubble. This also happens to be the sort of decline to which Mieno has publicly acknowledged. Since most banks claim never to have lent more than 70 percent of the equity value of a property, a 20 percent loss is considered a haircut lenders can afford to take. The reason for this sanguine attitude is the same one that most pundits, especially those living in Japan, used to put forward to explain why a stock market crash in Tokyo was impossible: Japan Inc. would never let it happen. Advocates of this view cite several structural or cultural factors that, they claim, make Japan's land market somehow immune from the cyclical swings suffered by other property markets. These factors deserve to be listed because they are so widely believed. First, many believe that Tokyo so dominates Japan's economy that there will always be demand for space in the city, where tight zoning and building regulations mean there will be a permanent land "shortage." Second, they point out that the tax system favors land. The effective landholding tax until the end of 1991 was a mere 0.07 percent of market value, in contrast to 4 percent in America. The tax system also discourages short-term trading of property. If land is sold within two years of its purchase then 150 percent of the capital gain is added to the seller's annual income and taxed accordingly. If sold within five years then 100 percent of the gain is added to income and taxed. This penal taxation is the major reason Japan's property market has traditionally been so illiquid, since people cannot afford the tax consequences of selling. It also means that Japan's property market is not the place to be a distressed seller. Third, experts argue that Japan is an immobile society where people hardly ever move. Any decline in the hypothetical resale value of a home is basically irrelevant because the owner is not going to sell anyway.

This last point leads directly to the favorite argument of the Japan-is-different school, though it is actually the Achilles's heel of the land bubble and the reason the system will now collapse under the twin blows of the huge increase in the cost of money in 1989 and 1990 and the central bank imposed withdrawal of credit to the property sector between April 1990 and the end of 1991. This argument is that the Japanese property market cannot collapse because there is no real market. If an individual has to sell land he sells it to a relative, which means that the supply of land never hits the market. Likewise, if a company's property subsidiary gets into trouble, its parent will take over the land and essentially warehouse it. Again, the supply will not hit the market and so there will be no downward pressure on prices.

This has indeed been a broadly accurate description of the condition of Japan's property market, at least until property companies from 1990 on began announcing their intention to sell property to reduce their debts. Robert Zielinski, a Tokyo-based financial analyst at the securities firm Jardine Fleming, sums up the state of play well. He says, "In Japan there is no real property market. Therefore you have no basis whatsoever of estimating how much property is worth." Zielinski views this as a sign of a hugely inefficient market and therefore the reason it is possible to make "huge profits in real estate." Sadly, the opposite may also be true, especially after a period of tight and even rationed credit. For if Japan's property market is as illiquid and as inefficient as says, which it is, then there is the risk of a downward spiral in values if land is forced on the market as credit rationing takes its toll. The best analogy is to compare Japan's property market to an unlisted privately placed security whose value is rarely tested because of the absence of a secondary market. The value of such securities is always greater in boom times because of their scarcity value. But when sentiment turns the decline in value is correspondingly that much worse precisely because of the lack of liquidity; prices have to fall that much farther before anyone is willing to buy.

An interesting study by Christofer Rathke, a fund manager with Union Bank of Switzerland's Tokyo-based trust banking subsidiary, illustrates the extent to which property became overvalued at the end of the 1980s even by traditional Japanese standards. He calculates that for most of the postwar period land prices have closely tracked economic growth. In the twenty years between 1965 and 1985 Japan's nominal GNP rose ten times, while land prices appreciated fivefold. However, since 1985 the ratio of land prices to GNP jumped to twice its average historical level. Rathke estimates that current prices, based on past historical values, discount seven years of 10 percent annual rates of nominal economic growth. Based on noninflationary growth of 5 percent, which has been more the pattern of late and is still a rather optimistic forecast for the immediate years ahead, it would take fifteen years for economic reality to catch up with current land values. This is a very long time indeed; it is far more likely that land prices will fall significantly to bring the trend line back to normal.

Rathke also notes that a fall in Japanese land values in real inflation-adjusted terms is not so extraordinary an event. City land prices fell 30 percent in real terms between 1973 and 1978. For the whole of the inflationary 1970s city land prices did not rise at all in real terms, even though real wages rose by 50 percent. In the deflationary 1990s it is most unlikely that inflation will bail out property owners and the banks that lent to them by reducing the real value of what is owed. Yet prices reached extreme levels. Condominium prices within a twelve-mile radius of Tokyo spiraled to more than ten times wage earners' average annual income. According to Rathke, the government's Housing Loan Corporation considers loans amounting to seven times annual income as close to the point of no return in terms of what a household can bear.

It is frightening that such a large amount of the world's available credit has been extended to a market that is so inefficient, so illiquid, and so overpriced. The banks that have made those loans have no secondary market to test the theoretical value of the land against which they have lent. Instead they have essentially made huge leaps of faith. Western analysts who do not consider this a problem put too much faith in Japan as some sort of special case immune from the natural cyclical laws that affect all markets. Perhaps the most extraordinary point of all is that so many of them have continued to subscribe to the myth of ever-rising house prices long after it has been demolished in the West.

Meanwhile, the evidence of trouble at property companies or companies involved with property continues to pile up. The first major casualty occurred in September 1990 when it was revealed that Itoman, the scandal-infested trading company, would have to be bailed out by its main bank, Sumitomo. Sumitomo had to take over some ¥500 billion of property loans made by Itoman (some of them to Itoman's own subsidiaries). Itoman's debt at the end of March 1990 was a cool eight times its shareholders' equity. This was only the first of many such stories as bankruptcies and debt reschedulings continued to rise inexorably throughout 1991. There has been a kind of pattern to the spreading bankruptcies. The first wave tended to involve comparative newcomers without main-bank relationships, what one wag calls "orphan companies." An example of this was Aoyama Building Development, which went bust with total debts of ¥110 billion in January 1991. Aoyama was set up in 1987 and had an annual turnover of only ¥8.5 billion for the year ending September 1989. It failed after it was unable to sell land in central Tokyo that it thought was worth a theoretical ¥40 billion. The next wave of failures featured companies that had become active in resort development. One example is Kyowa, a steel bridge builder that diversified disastrously into golf course development. It failed with debts of ¥200 billion. Kyowa later became famous for its involvement in a political scandal that at the beginning of 1992 led to the arrest of Fumio Abe, a former cabinet minister and close political associate of prime minister Kiichi Miyazawa. Kyowa was said to have doled out ¥2.2 billion to politicians, including ¥480 million to Abe. In return, prosecutors allege that Abe gave the firm details of where a new road was to be built on Hokkaido, Japan's northernmost island. Abe was the minister in charge of Hokkaido development at the time. The mere fact of money being handed out to politicians was hardly shocking. The word from political insiders was that Abe was only caught because he had been unbelievably sloppy in not disguising the transaction by using dummy companies and the like. Still, the episode showed how companies caught up in the bubble were tempted to play politics. Another bankruptcy involved Nanatomi, a resort developer that failed in January 1991 with debts of ¥286 billion. The Nanatomi debacle exposed the risky though widespread practice whereby Japanese construction companies had procured business. In exchange for orders, contractors would lend property companies money or guarantee their loans. Thus, when Nanatomi went into receivership, it emerged that Tobishima, a major construction firm, had extended ¥106 billion of loan guarantees to the developer. In return the contractor had ¥40 billion of outstanding orders from Nanatomi.

As the property market has deteriorated it has increasingly hurt more established property developers. The collapse of Maruko in August 1991 with debts of ¥278 billion was the first failure of a property concern listed on the stock market (in this case the over-the-counter market). It was also the first time that a Japanese company had defaulted on equity-linked bonds issued in the Euro-markets. Maruko was founded in 1975 and was a pioneer in developing a peculiarly Japanese form of residential property known rather oddly as "one-room mansion apartments." When trouble hit, Maruko's main bank, Mitsubishi Trust, moved its own team into the property company to devise a way of saving it. However, the bankers decided to let the company go when Maruko leaked the details of its version of a proposed rescheduling to the press before Mitsubishi Trust had agreed to it. In Japan, the banks retain the upper hand in such circumstances.

If there have been plenty of casualties to date (and bankruptcies in Japan totaled ¥8 trillion in 1991 with every prospect that the 1992 figure will be higher), it is nevertheless true that the property companies that are reckoned to be the biggest potential failures have yet to bite the dust. In Tokyo talk centers on four companies that are known by the collective nickname of AIDS: Azabu Building, EIE International, Dai-Ichi Real Estate, and Shuwa Corporation. EIE is a ward of LTCB, and Azabu Building and Dai-Ichi are wards of Mitsui Trust. The latter is a bank that, despite its illustrious name, has made more than its fair share of loans to shady property companies and, at best, will emerge from the current crisis with its reputation and capital considerably reduced.

Shuwa is Japan's fourth-largest property company. It bought most of its Japanese properties before the boom. A private company, it became during the bubble years a big-time stock market speculator and then a big-time investor in American property. It owns scores of properties in America including the ABC Building, a landmark in Manhattan. Shuwa's total group debts are put at around ¥1.3 trillion. An attempt to restructure Azabu Building, which has group debts of ¥700 billion, was announced in February 1992. They hope to sell nearly ¥300 billion worth of property. At the same time, Toshimi Shibata, a former Mitsui Trust executive, was installed as president of the company. He replaced Kitaro Watanabe, Azabu's autocratic chief. Watanabe is famous for financing Texan investor T. Boone Pickens's much-publicized 1989 purchase of 42 million shares, or 26.4 percent, of Koito Manufacturing, a manufacturer of auto components and part of the Toyota group. Azabu Building is now sitting on these Koito shares at a huge loss. In January an attempt by Azabu Building to sell its Koito shares to a Swedish investment company broke down, leaving Mitsui Trust with the task of trying to find a buyer at an acceptable price. Koito's shares peaked at ¥5,470 in March 1989. They were ¥2,130 in February 1992.

In Osaka there is another group of talked-about companies, known as FOKAS: Fuji Juken, Ogisaka, Kawabe Bussan, Asahi Juken, and Sueno Kosan. Ogisaka was the first casualty, going bust in early 1991. The amount of debt that had been taken on by some of these companies amazes even insiders in the property industry. In October 1991 it emerged that Fuji Juken, a none-too-special Osaka-based condominium maker, was in discussion with its banks about how to reschedule its group debt of ¥834 billion. This is a huge exposure for a company that reported revenues of only ¥160 billion in 1990. Japan's biggest bankruptcy so far was the ¥520 billion failure of Sanko Steamship, a shipping company, in 1985; it is a record that Fuji Juken will soon break. Asahi Juken, though Japan's second-largest condominium developer in 1990, has no clear main bank relationship. This presented a problem when the company could no longer service its debt, since it was too big to be allowed to fail. The pragmatic solution was to bring in the trading company C. Itoh to manage Asahi Juken's restructuring in cooperation with the major bank creditors. The trading company had a personal interest since it was in business with the condominium developer. This is an example of Japanese-style crisis management at work. It helped prevent, or at least delay, a nasty surprise and the dumping of Asahi Juken's properties on the market.

These are examples of some of the bigger speculative companies whose names only became familiar during the Bubble Economy and whose exact origins and sources of financing were often unclear. However, the pain does not end there. Signs of distress have even reached the best capitalized property companies, the blue chips of the sector. In September 1991 Mitsui Real Estate, Japan's largest property company in terms of revenues, said it proposed to sell six Tokyo office rental buildings in 1991 and 1992 to raise a hoped-for ¥40 billion. Putting six buildings up for sale in a single year in a depressed market is unusual for Mitsui and is a sure sign the company needs to raise cash. Another indication of a weakening market was a plan announced by Mitsui in late 1991 to "securitize" (sell shares to investors) an office building in the Tsukiji district of Tokyo, near the Ginza. The interesting point is less the technique than the price at which Mitsui was prepared to sell. The company estimated that investors who bought at the asking price would earn an annual return on their capital of 4 percent, which happened to be almost double the rental yield (between 2 and 2.5 percent) that until then was normally reckoned to apply to central Tokyo office buildings. The implication was again that property was worth at least 30 percent less than official figures showed. Securitization is a relative novelty in Japan. Some 14,000 securitized property units have been sold there, representing an investment value of ¥310 billion. The first deal was done in the spring of 1987 in Tokyo by a subsidiary of Mitsui. The unfortunates who bought into that deal receive an annual yield of only 1.7 percent.

Even the best of the blue-chip companies are feeling the strain of rationed bank loans and sagging stock markets and have joined the long list of firms that have publicly announced their intention to sell. Yet, revealingly, there are desperately few examples of troubled companies that have announced the successful sale of a property, let alone what they sold it for.

The final blow for land prices could be a change in official policy toward land. After years of completely ignoring the problem the government is now, officially at least, committed to lowering land prices. One result was a series of tax changes introduced in early 1992. Despite much fanfare the effect of these changes was almost counterproductive. True, a new landholding tax was introduced, to be levied from 1993 on at a rate of 0.3 percent of the so-called assessment value, which itself is about 70 percent of official land prices. This is not so onerous since those levied will only be paying 0.8 to 1 percent of their property's market value each year, which by way of comparison is around a fifteenth to a tenth of the share for which Californians (who have had a lid on property tax increases for the past thirteen years) are liable. Moreover, most people will not have to pay the tax. All residential plots of less than 1,000 square meters (about one-quarter acre) are exempt. That means virtually everybody since a plot of that size is equivalent to a country estate in crowded Japan.

Though the tax on property is hardly oppressive, the increase in the tax on capital gains from selling property will be harder to bear. There is now an effective tax rate of 90 percent on the capital gain from the sale of a property owned for less than two years. This falls to a still-punitive 75 percent on the sale of a property owned for between two and five years. Property held for more than five years incurs a tax rate of more than 50 percent when sold. Ostensibly this tough new tax is designed to deter property speculation. In reality the effect will be counterproductive since it will only further constrain supply. By raising the tax cost of selling, the new law further discourages anyone from selling, save the most distressed owners who simply have to raise cash. Given this fact, it is a sign of just how dire conditions are that so many property companies have already announced their intention to sell. One reason must be that an increasing number of them will be selling recently purchased buildings at a loss, or selling buildings to offset the gains against losses they have taken on other properties.

The crash promises to be a drawn-out affair that will take several years to reach bottom, which needs to happen before a genuine recovery can occur. The prevailing view within the property industry is that it will take between three and five years because developers and the banks that have lent to them will exhaust every option in the hope of hanging on for the recovery in prices, and so containing the problem within the banking system, before resorting to the final option of selling in the open market.

Land prices in Japan have traditionally been held up by an unholy trinity of physical scarcity, feudal tradition, and perverse government policies. Japan's property market would suffer an even more precipitous decline if the government ever did away with the various artificial props to the market that combine to make land far more expensive than need be. The most important government interventions involve zoning regulations, agricultural protectionism, and confiscatory taxation. These policies entail a risk for property owners, though many are not aware of it. For anyone who invests in Japanese property today makes a rather heroic assumption that the government will continue to support the artificial props that prevent the property market from clearing at a far more rational and lower level. This is a big bet, one a prudent man would not make. Demographic trends are running against the status quo as more and more members of a falling population discover they cannot afford to own their homes and are forced to rent instead. It also is unhealthy, to say the least, for Japan to have so much of its national wealth locked up unrealized in land, or borrowed against it in speculative ventures. The economic distortions and resulting devastation wrought by the Bubble Economy is the best example of just how unhealthy it is.

It is not difficult to come up with the sort of policies that would free up Japan's property market. They can best be described as supply-side shocks. Perhaps the quickest and simplest way to bring down land prices sharply would be a radical cut in the capital gains tax to 20 percent or even zero—regardless of how long land has been owned. This would allow owners of property to make rational economic decisions; to sell if it suited their financial self-interest and switch the funds into other investment assets, be they shares, bonds, or cash. Right now the vast majority of owners never sell simply because they would have to pay so much tax if they did. This tax burden also applies when passing assets between the generations. Inheritance tax is a major obsession for all Japanese with wealth to protect, with good reason. If a person's assets at death are valued at more than ¥500 million, his heirs have to find 70 percent of that in cash to pay the tax man. Assets worth between ¥250 million and ¥500 million incur an almost as stiff tax rate of 65 percent. A sum of ¥500 million may sound like a lot, but in the loony world of Japanese land values it is not. Until 1990 the pain was alleviated somewhat because inheritance tax was levied on assessments at only about 50 percent of real market value. Now it is assessed on some 70 percent of market value. Few Japanese, practically none in the middle class, can lay their hands on the cash needed to meet such tax bills. So they sell the land, or at least part of it, to pay the tax. Consequently, Japan is becoming divided into ever smaller plots. Since land is still revered as the ultimate store of value, every effort is made to hang on to a piece of dirt, however tiny, to pass on to the next generation.

The horrors of the inheritance tax are highlighted in a tax case that was reported in the Japanese press in November 1991. The case concerned four relatives of Kenshiro Otsuka, a Tokyo landlord who died in 1990. They claimed they inherited ¥11.8 billion worth of properties, shares, and other taxable assets. However, the tax authorities disputed the value put on a building near Tokyo's Ikebukuro Station. The heirs declared a value of ¥6.1 billion based on National Land Agency official prices. Their problem was that the tax man found a contract Otsuka had signed with a property company at the peak of the market that valued his property at ¥15.1 billion. This promopted the tax authorities to demand another ¥3.7 billion in tax, which is a lot of cash to come up with suddenly. This episode also serves to show the huge gulf between National Land Agency "official" prices and market reality. During the Bubble Economy these official prices did not keep up with market appreciation. Now, as prices crash, the official prices dramatically underestimate the extent of the decline.

The easing of height restrictions on buildings and the rezoning of land are other obvious ways to increase supply and reduce prices. Tokyo has very few skyscrapers for a city of its scale, while more than 5 percent of Tokyo's land is still zoned for agriculture. There are still 89,000 acres of farmland and 56,000 acres of vacant land in the greater Tokyo area, which in a free market could be sold for billions of dollars. One reason for this absurdity is that taxes levied on Tokyo land classified as agricultural were, until a partial reform introduced in early 1992, even lower than normal taxes so long as crops (a cabbage patch or an apple tree counts) are grown. So "crops" were grown, not for any economic value, but because they qualified the owner, usually a part-time "urban farmer," for special tax treatment. Such crude protection of farmers' special interests cannot last much longer, if only because the older, more rural generation is dying off. The political system will increasingly represent the urban salaried worker whose overwhelming interest will be for more affordable housing and so a greater supply of it.

The reluctance to sell land, and the resulting lack of supply and continuing subdivision into ever smaller plots, makes it very hard for developers to assemble land into large sites, because agreements have to be separately negotiated with numerous smallholders. It took Mori, for example, fifteen years to assemble the Arkhills site in Akasaka in central Tokyo. Even now this commercial development still has fifty-seven small minority shareholders. This is why large urban sites are so rare in Japan. It also is why they are so valuable. A foreigners' window on the idiosyncrasies of the Tokyo property market is provided by K. K. Halifax, a joint venture between Hong Kong's Jardine Matheson and America's Pacific Architects and Engineers. It is one of the longest established foreign-owned property development companies working in Japan and has been active there for more than twenty years. During the course of developing a site near Tokyo's Yasukuni Shrine (where Japan's war heroes are memorialized) Halifax spent seven years negotiating with an old woman who lived in a small traditional wooden house on part of the proposed site. In the end the developer could not offer the owner any incentive attractive enough to induce her to move, and so had to build around her house. Selling the land outright would have incurred too much tax; if the woman avoided the tax by buying another property she would have ended up living much farther from the urban center than she was prepared to.

Another constraint to supply that could easily be legislated away is Japan's almost socialistic rent controls. A tenant has very strong rights of occupation, which may even extend beyond the life of the building he occupies. Leases are effectively renewable in-definitely at the tenant's option, while rent increases are capped for existing tenants. Consequently, as in all markets with rent control, new tenants subsidize old ones, further distorting the market.

So much can be done to make Japanese property more afford-able. The danger is that social and political pressures will cause these secular changes to be introduced at the same time as the abrupt rationing of credit is causing the century's biggest cyclical bust in Japanese property prices. That convergence of structural and cyclical forces would amount to a savage double blow for the world's biggest asset market and result in a huge markdown in the value of the collateral underpinning the country's banking system.

Demographics also cannot be ignored. The 1.2 million Japa-nese live births in 1990 was the lowest number recorded since 1893. By comparison, the 1979 figure was 1.66 million. Even worse, growth in the so-called active population, aged between fifteen and sixty-four, is decelerating rapidly. It is reckoned that during the 1990s, for the first time in the statistical history of Japan, this population group will show no increase at all. David Shulman, head of real estate research at Salomon Brothers in New York and one of the few property analysts to have predicted Amer-ica's commercial property slump, argues convincingly that struc-tural constraints such as extraordinarily high house prices and crowded living conditions are a major, if not the main, reason why Japanese people have stopped having children. The logical implica-tion is that the land market needs to be freed up to encourage

Japanese couples to start having larger families again. Yet such a supply-side shock puts at risk the banking system and, with it, the flow of credit throughout the economy. This is Japan's dilemma. It is the reason Japanese property prices are not again likely to reach the peak levels seen in the late 1980s until the beginning of the next century at the earliest.

# 4

# Life Insurance Companies

At some point during all great stock market declines, the animal spirits begin to panic. So it was in Tokyo in September 1990. With the Nikkei index down nearly 50 percent on the year and no relief in sight, rumors swept through the market about how much farther prices had to fall before the share portfolios of all Japan's life insurance companies would show net losses.

This possibility would have been inconceivably remote just one year earlier. During the 1980s, Japan's twenty-five life insurance companies, with total reported assets of ¥130 trillion as of March 31, 1991, came to symbolize the country's raw financial power. These are even more conservative institutions than the banks, and certainly much more averse to risk. They symbolize permanence and security. They own more Japanese shares than any other type of financial institution, owning 13 percent of the Tokyo stock market at the end of March 1990, compared with 9 percent held by city banks, the next biggest shareholders. Life insurers have also been active overseas investors in recent years. They accounted for up to 60 percent of Japan's enormous capital outflows during the 1980s, much of which flowed into American Treasury bonds and (in lesser though growing proportions) into other sorts of bonds and shares.

So important have the life insurance companies been in providing a level of price support to Japanese stocks, not to mention American Treasury bonds and sundry other financial instruments worldwide, that any suggestion of net losses on their stock portfolios could trigger global panic. It could even cause Japanese policyholders to cash in their policies, prompting investors to dump stocks in anticipation of life insurance company selling.

Japan's life insurers are mutually owned companies with no shareholders to report to. Because they want to avoid just such a panic they are not disclosing the average cost of their stock portfolios, even though being mutual companies, these capital gains belong to their policyholders, not the companies themselves. Still, based on industry-wide figures it is estimated that all capital gains would be wiped out if the Nikkei declined to 12,500. Although this is still far below recent lows such a decline is not outside the realm of possibility. Based on the March 1993 company earnings forecast of Barclays De Zoete Wedd (BZW), a British securities firm, the Japanese stock market would still be selling on a prospective price-earnings ratio of 20 should the Nikkei index fall to 10,000. That compares with a price-earnings ratio of 47 (also based on BZW's forecast) with the Nikkei at 24,000. There is thus plenty of scope for further declines should matters turn nasty.

Few people have examined this issue in detail, mainly because conventional wisdom views it as alarmist and fanciful. However, Timothy Griffen, a fund manager formerly with Cigna International in Tokyo, concluded in an asset-liability study of the insurance industry in Japan that the real condition of most life insurers is worse than the gross figures suggest. He calculated that the average cost of shares held for most life insurers is nearer 18,000 on the Nikkei than 12,500. Certainly some of the smaller life insurance companies were already under water when the Nikkei fell to 21,000. The average is probably being dragged down by the sheer size of Nippon Life; with its assets of ¥27 trillion at the end of March 1991, it accounts for nearly one-quarter of the industry. Nippon probably has a lower average cost because being so big (it owns 3 percent of the whole stock market) it has already reached its statutory 5 percent shareholding limit in many companies. That would have prevented it from buying more shares at recently in-flated prices. Haruaki Deguchi, a senior manager in Nippon Life's investment-planning department, says that at about 12,000 on the Nikkei, Nippon Life would be at the point of breaking even. But he regards such considerations as entirely academic. "The 15,000 level [on the Nikkei] will never occur again," he asserted bravely in a conversation in September 1990.

The more aggressive a life insurance company has been in recent years in its investment strategy, the higher the average cost of its shares and the more vulnerable it now is. Though these companies may own lots of Nippon Steel shares purchased for, say, ¥50 in 1950, they have bought so many more shares at inflated prices during the late 1980s that the average cost of their equity holdings has soared. In 1984, when the Nikkei hovered around 10,000, the life insurance industry had 10 percent of its assets invested in Japanese equities. By the end of 1989, the peak of the bull market, it had 26 percent invested in Japanese equities (includ-ing *tokkin* accounts, of which more later). During this same period life insurance companies' assets grew from ¥45 trillion (April 1985) to ¥116 trillion (March 31, 1990), a level of expansion unparalleled in the industry's history.

That headlong expansion is now over. As with the banks, asset growth has now collapsed. The life insurance industry, which still operates like a cartel, paying out the same guaranteed rates of return to policyholders (plus a dividend bonus based on investment performance), must now face the consequences of interest rate deregulation and, in particular, having to compete with banks of-fering savers a better deal. Life insurers have also in recent years been hit by massive redemptions of formerly popular but increas-ingly uncompetitive savings policies. That has caused a severe decline in companies' asset growth, intensifying the cash crunch now occurring throughout Japan.

Like the banks, the life insurers clung for too long to the belief that asset growth was good in itself. They ignored the need to prepare for deregulation and adapt institutional behavior accord-ingly. Instead the life insurance industry continued to sell products designed for a more regulated world through their army of 400,000 salesmen, many of them women in their early forties.

The big boom in the mid-1980s came from sales of single-premium endowment policies, particularly five-year lump-sum savings plans. These policies have nothing to do with traditional life insurance. At a time when the banks still could not offer money-market rates to most depositors, these policies guaranteed a minimum rate of return of 6.2 percent plus dividends at a time when interest rates in Japan were as low as 3 percent. There were minimal redemption penalties on such policies, and the money poured into them between 1984 and 1988. Then two things happened. First, under pressure from the banks, the finance ministry forced the life insurance companies to reduce the attractiveness of these savings policies. Second, the banks themselves were increasingly able to offer more competitive savings products as interest rates were deregulated. Money began flowing the other way—out of the life insurers and into the banks.

Life insurers now face a dramatic decline in their asset growth. After averaging more than 20 percent annual growth in the late 1980s, life insurance companies' asset growth will collapse, since most of the ¥10 trillion of savings policies that come due between 1990 and 1994 will not be renewed. The fiscal year that ended March 1991 was the first year since 1945 that the life insurance industry suffered a decline in asset growth. Total assets grew by only 11.5 percent. Nippon Life calculates that in the fiscal year ended March 1992 the industry's asset growth will be 10 percent, but that may prove too optimistic. McKinsey, the management consulting firm, predicts only 5 percent asset growth, while Griffen concluded in his study that asset growth in 1992 could actually turn negative in life insurance companies' general accounts.

Such an outcome would cause the life insurers to be faced with net negative cash flow, in the sense that net premiums and interest income they received would be less than the funds they paid out. This is hugely important. Since 1945 Japan's life insurance industry has been successfully meeting its obligations on a cash-flow basis thanks to regular annual double-digit asset growth. The

companies, which are happy to be subsidized by long-term policy-holders in the general accounts and which like the guarantee against losses implied by life insurers' still quite considerable level of unrealized capital gains. Trust banks, already loaded to the gills with problem property debts and sitting on big losses on their various stock market investment vehicles, are livid at what they view rightly as the life insurers' unfair advantage in the pension business. But reform may be some way off. It is true that the finance ministry is considering introducing what officials refer to as "internal segmented accounts" within the life insurers' general accounts. This sounds like a contradiction in terms, since it seems to mean separating each major line of business, be it conventional life insurance or pensions. But this is only one small part of a broad effort at reforming the insurance industry that began in 1989 and, in typical Japanese style, could rumble on for another three or four more years.

Still, it is clear that life insurers have boosted their returns on pension accounts by writing up the value of some old stock holdings. Officially, life insurers increased their stock portfolios by some ¥3.4 trillion in the year ending March 1991. Yet Tokyo Stock Exchange data show they were modest net sellers during that period. The increase in the values of their portfolios came from the rise in the average cost of some of their holdings, through what is known as "booking up." Such smoothing out of returns entails a cost. There are now fewer profits left to carry forward for next year, especially since life insurers' stock portfolios were already devastated by Tokyo's stock market crash. Nippon Life calculates that life insurers' unrealized profits on shares are now only about 25 percent of their total assets, compared with 50 percent at the end of 1989.

The inflow of corporate pension money will help to keep overall asset growth marginally positive for the life insurers, even though the process of booking up artificially inflates that growth. For example, asset growth would have been 9 percent, instead of 12 percent, in the year ended March 1991 if revaluation of stocks through booking up is excluded. Certainly, any sudden lurch into negative cash flow would be doubly painful for the life insurers because of the generosity of those single-premium endowment policies that were so popular a few years ago. The life insurance companies could only offer those returns, which were way above anything that could be earned on deposit in Japan at the time, by resorting to two sorts of financial gimmickry, both of which resulted from a quirk of Japanese accounting law that states that life insurance companies can only pay policyholders out of income, not out of capital gains.

First, life insurance companies set up special *tokkin* accounts. These are a form of trust account where money is wagered for short-term gains in the stock market. *Tokkin* exploded in size as a result of tax law changes. These special accounts enabled both financial institutions and corporate investors to separate profitably, for tax purposes, short-term holdings of shares bought as a gamble from their long-term, seldom-traded cross-shareholdings in companies, which are owned for reasons of business relationships. *Tokkin* assets peaked with the stock market at ¥43 trillion at the end of 1989. At least one-third of this amount was invested in stocks. Life insurers were allowed by the finance ministry to invest first 3 percent of their total assets and (after January 1988 in a deliberate and successful ploy to help revive the stock market following the worldwide October 1987 crash) then 5 percent of their total assets in *tokkin*. The specific lure of *tokkin* was that it enabled the life insurance companies to convert capital gains into income free of tax and so pay policyholders out of the proceeds. Japan's stock market crash ended that convenience. In October 1990, in another blatant effort to boost the stock market, the finance ministry again raised the amount of life insurance companies' assets that could be invested in *tokkin* from 5 percent to 7 percent. The snag was that on this occasion the life insurers did not take the bait. With most *tokkin* funds by then already heavily under water, with a book value of around 30,000 on the Nikkei index, the last thing life insurers wanted to do was to buy more shares. Indeed, with no more capital gains to convert to income, some life insurance companies had resorted to hedging their *tokkin* exposure secretly by selling stock index futures. That way, if the market continued to fall they could at least report the capital gain made by selling futures. Never mind that the underlying shares would be worth even less.

The second way life insurance companies during the boom sought to pay returns way above those available in yen short-term deposits or bonds was through high-yielding investments overseas. Again, the fact that policyholders can only be paid out of income, not capital gains, prompted some weird investing. Aided by smart Western investment bankers who made it their profitable business to understand their clients' strange needs, life insurers pursued high income at all costs, almost regardless of the risk of loss of capital. The result was a bewildering array of financial gymnastics as foreign bankers served up instruments that paid high running yields and virtually no principal at maturity.

Life insurance companies were not concerned about the risk of loss in overseas investing because, like the banks, they had a huge portfolio of unrealized capital gains from the shares they held in their general accounts. The theory was that any capital or currency losses sustained in overseas investing could be offset by those unrealized gains in the booming Tokyo stock market, capital gains that could not be used (unlike profits in *tokkin* accounts) to pay out policyholders.

The overseas expansion was always a gamble for the life insurers because most of them were entering an investment world about which they had scant knowledge and in which they had almost zero experience. Traditionally, top management at the life insurance companies has come from the marketing, not the investment, side of the business. The emphasis has been on gathering assets through the vast sales network, not on how those assets should be invested. However, the rush of money invested overseas, which took off in earnest in 1983 as Japan's current account surplus built up, increasingly raised the importance of the fund manager within these organizations, especially those posted to the suddenly glamorous area of international investment.

The life insurers were starting from considerable ignorance, since the investment divisions were unsophisticated to say the least. An American who joined Sumitomo Life, Japan's third-largest life insurer, in 1985 straight from college recalls that at that time there was not a personal computer in sight in the entire investment department. Instead, a woman would come in daily and spend a couple of hours with a calculator working out the balance of various portfolios. As for buying and selling, it was not uncommon for domestic fund managers to be visited by Japanese brokers in their own offices. The brokers would sit down next to them, tout stocks and, when successful, literally telephone in their orders. This practice obviously raises questions of gross conflicts of interest and illustrates the extent to which investment practices went unregulated.

The life insurers had a lot to learn in a hurry about the world of international investment when they were suddenly faced with all this cash to spend. It was not just a question of mastering modern investment techniques. It also meant getting used to operating in a non-yen world. Investing overseas meant that the life insurers had to contend with enormous currency risks. This contrasts with the experiences of Japan's British and American predecessors when their countries ran vast capital surpluses with the rest of the world (Britain in the 1870s and America in the 1950s). These two countries were able to invest their money in essentially sterling and dollar worlds. The Japanese were not so fortunate. Each time they invested money overseas they assumed a foreign-exchange risk, there being no substantial investment outlets in offshore yen. This posed an enormous dilemma, which was also without precedent. At no time in history has a country ever had to assume such foreign-exchange risks with such a large body of assets from which it hoped to derive its future prosperity.

The expansion into investing overseas was fraught with risk, and it has since backfired to a large extent. The question now is to what extent the losses sustained by the life insurers' overseas investing have wiped out what is left of their shrunken capital gains at home. Unfortunately, no one outside the life insurance companies knows the answer because disclosure is not required and they, naturally, are not telling. Still, some of the losses overseas have been substantial, especially since in the earlier years the life insurers did not bother to hedge their currency risk. For example, in the financial year ended March 31, 1987, the life insurance companies reported currency losses of ¥2.24 trillion. The top seven companies wrote off ¥1.7 trillion between them. Overall, between 1985 and 1989 the entire life insurance industry lost about ¥5 trillion on currency movements. Griffen suspects that foreign losses have probably wiped out outstanding capital gains on share portfolios to a far greater extent than is commonly realized.

Because life insurance companies are not publicly quoted, and therefore not analyzed to death by stock specialists, their pressing problems are not nearly as well understood as those of the banks, where public scrutiny is intense. Yet the consequences of the Ponzi scheme becoming unglued are immense. If Japan is in the midst of an implosion of financial institutions' balance sheets, as yesterday's property and share-backed credit inflation turns into today's asset deflation, the most vulnerable institutions will be those that expanded their balance sheets the most during the boom. The life insurance companies are more firmly in this category than even the banks. Also, their assets are relatively illiquid. Some 38 percent of their assets were in domestic loans, many of them backed by property, at the end of March 1991, and another 6 percent was invested directly in property. Yet their liabilities, in the form of endowment policies that are easily surrendered, can all too easily walk out the door.

Some life insurance companies may be forced to sell shares at a loss to meet policyholder claims. For the 25 percent of their assets that were invested in Japanese equities on March 31, 1991 (including *tokkin* accounts), represent one of their more liquid (i.e., salable) assets. This is one reason why life insurance companies' ownership of Japanese shares as a percentage of their assets has probably reached a cyclical peak, and why the industry will in the next few years be a net seller of equities. There are two other reasons. First, life insurers are fed up with the measly returns, in the form of minuscule dividends, they receive on Japanese shares.

Second, they do not expect the Tokyo stock market to be a very exciting performer. Nippon Life's Deguchi voices a common opinion when he says he does not expect the Nikkei index to rise more than 6 or 8 percent annually in the next five years. That is a far cry from the rate of return both enjoyed and expected during the 1980s. This lackluster outlook also explains why Nippon Life expects life insurers to have only 20 percent of their assets in Japanese stocks by 1995, down from the present 25 percent. A five percentage point drop may not sound like a lot, but it is big money to the life insurers. It is certainly not good news for the Tokyo stock market that its largest group of institutional investors plans to be a net seller of shares in the first half of the decade. Nor for that matter is Nippon Life bullish on the property market. It expects the life insurance industry to have 5 percent of its assets invested in land and buildings in 1995, down from 5.5 percent in March 1991. In a forecast issued in January 1992, Nippon Life's research institute predicted that it would take three to four years for the property market to recover.

Japan's cash crunch will also have the effect of propelling the long cartelized life insurance industry into the late twentieth century. Weaker players will be forced to merge with stronger companies and, as has already happened in America and Britain, some life insurers will be forced by financial pressures to go public to raise capital. Also, as occurred in America and Britain in the 1970s, life insurance companies will increasingly seek to shift investment risk off their own balance sheets by moving funds from the general account into separate accounts. A hint that the authorities sense trouble ahead came in a development reported at the beginning of 1992. The finance ministry is considering introducing some form of safety net for policyholders that would be tapped in the event of an insurance company's failure.

These are the longer-term consequences. Shorter term, life insurance companies ended their love affair with overseas investing in 1990 as they rushed to bring their money back home. Their money was needed in Japan to make up for the drastic slowdown in bank lending, and by 1990 they could once again earn sensible returns in yen cash, yen bonds, and yen domestic loans. With interest rates having risen under the Bank of Japan's tight monetary policy, the life insurers could buy bonds and comfortably earn the 6 percent return they needed to meet their obligations to their policyholders without taking any currency or investment risks, assuming they held the bonds until maturity.

As a consequence, in 1991 life insurers allocated about 60 percent of their cash flow to domestic loans. In so doing they were taking up some of the slack left by the contracting banking sector. In fact, the life insurers found they could not lend all the money they had allocated. They did not want to lend to those troubled sectors that badly needed to borrow, namely nonbanks and property and construction firms. But the companies they did want to lend to, creditworthy manufacturing and service firms, increasingly did not want to borrow as they reduced their capital spending plans and generally turned cautious in the face of a weakening economy. Meanwhile, overseas investment fell off sharply. The amount of money life insurers invested overseas in 1990 was 60 percent below 1989's level. This is why the 17 percent of their total assets invested in foreign securities on March 31, 1990, probably marks a cyclical peak, the high point of Japan's wave of overseas investment. In 1989 Japan's total net overseas portfolio was $114 billion. In the first eight months of 1990 it fell to $39 billion. Life insurance companies still feel they own too many foreign securities. While they were once only too happy to take big risks, they are now correspondingly that much cautious.

Life insurers will now become more vociferous about getting paid a proper dividend yield on their Japanese shares, and so will act increasingly like institutional investors in America and Europe. Indeed, they have already made a start in this respect. This will mark the beginning of the end of Japan's cross-shareholding system. Such a system only makes sense when it is based on mutual benefit. For the life insurance companies this has increasingly not been the case. During the bull market they could not issue equity because they were not public companies. Yet they were expected, for example, to buy all the banks' equity issues however microscopic the dividend yield. The life insurance companies have already expressed their displeasure with this unsatisfactory status quo. Dai-Ichi Life, the second-largest life insurer, announced in 1991 that it would reduce its long-term holdings in the Bank of Tokyo, Mitsui Taiyo Kobe Bank, and the Industrial Bank of Japan. The banks will be the key losers in this gradual unraveling of cross-shareholdings because they were the prime beneficiaries of the system. Companies bought their shares for access to credit. This is why at the peak of the stock market in 1989 only an estimated 8 percent of bank shares traded freely, with the rest tied up in supposedly long-term holdings. This narrow float, and the correspondingly small amount of available stock to investors, was a major reason why bank shares became so overvalued. That this situation will now reverse itself as life insurers and others sell low-yielding and still overvalued bank shares is another reason why the banks face a long-term decline in the value of their shares, and why the Tokyo stock market faces structural problems.

# 5

# Securities Companies

It was perhaps the classic case of Japanese hubris, 1980s style. It was a two-page Nomura advertisement run in the international print media at the end of 1988. The advertisement was headlined "Copernicus and Ptolemy." It compared ever-bullish Nomura's outlook on the Japanese stock market with the views propounded by Copernicus, the fifteenth-century philosopher who taught the world that the planets revolve around the sun. The ad went on to deride as present-day followers of Ptolemy (the Greek-Egyptian second-century mathematician and committed flat earther) the skeptics "who point to sky high prices and claim that Tokyo is much too expensive and that the market is unstable . . . instead of deepening their knowledge and enlightening themselves with the Copernican point of view." It ended with the immortal phrase "Copernicus or Ptolemy? Enlighten yourself."

Less than two years later, the mood had changed drastically. Just how drastically was clear from a strange incident that occurred in September 1990. A group of Japanese pundits were discussing on television where they thought the stock market was heading. Oddly, the pundits' faces were fuzzed out, like drug dealers, rape victims, or mafiosi turned government witnesses. No one in group-think Japan wanted the dishonor (sorry, loss of face) of being associated with a declining market.

Such extraordinary behavior explains the part embarrassment, part shame felt by so many individuals and so many companies at losing money in the stock market. This trauma threatens to put them off investing in shares for several years to come, which would be bad news for Japan's securities companies, which were among the prime beneficiaries, financially, of the Bubble Economy.

Japan's stockbrokers have been hit hard by the market's collapse. Profits for the Big Four securities houses—Nomura, Daiwa, Nikko, and Yamaichi—fell by some 60 percent in 1990. Smaller securities companies more reliant on the individual investor saw bigger falls of 80 percent and worse. Life got even tougher the next year. In 1991 virtually every broker save Nomura lost money. Even though the absolute level of the stock market did not sink to new lows, trading volume continued to decline as the bear market doldrums set in and as the securities scandals undermined investors' confidence. The average daily trading volume on the Tokyo Stock Exchange in 1991 was one-third of the levels seen in 1989. This was a major blow for the securities firms, nearly all of which still derive most of their profits from commission income. The forty-seven largest securities firms recorded aggregate losses of ¥34.2 billion between March and September 1991. Yamaichi, the fourth-largest broker, actually lost money during this period, while Nikko, the third largest and the securities arm of the powerful Mitsubishi group, reported pretax profits of only ¥12 billion. This was less than the Japanese subsidiaries of Morgan Stanley and Salomon Brothers, two of America's premier investment banks, who reported to the finance ministry pretax profits of ¥13 billion and ¥16 billion, respectively. This signaled an unprecedented success for foreign firms in Japan's domestic securities market and only added to the local brokers' misery.

The pain is far from over. If the bear market continues for much longer many of the 270-odd securities firms in Japan will go out of business or be swallowed up by larger entities, prompting massive consolidation and waves of mergers throughout the industry. One buyer could be the banks, assuming the finance ministry lets them in the game. Banks are now only allowed to own up to

5 percent of a securities firm. That sort of restriction will not survive a prolonged bear market. Still, it would be wrong to think it is all gloom and doom, at least for the very biggest securities firms. Their scandal-infested industry may be in the midst of a grim slump, but they have one often-ignored point going in their favor as the bubble bursts. Unlike many of their clients, be they banks, insurance companies, industrial companies, or individual investors, the securities companies managed to keep most of the enormous profits they made during the bull market. They also are for the most part shielded from credit risk, an important point as the Japanese liquidity boom implodes on itself.

Nomura, Japan's and the world's largest stockbroking firm and the company at the center of the securities scandals that erupted in the summer of 1991, is the prime example of the profits that could be made. It enjoyed stunning success in the late 1980s. Founded in Osaka in 1925 as a spinoff from Daiwa Bank's bond department, Nomura was the most profitable financial institution in the world in 1987 and also the most profitable company in Japan, overtaking for the first time such industrial giants as Tokyo Electric Power and Toyota. That year Nomura reported pretax profits of ¥494 billion. This performance was reflected in Nomura's stock, which appreciated 900 percent between 1983 and 1987 as its pretax profits rose fourfold. At its peak of ¥5,990 per share on April 20, 1987, Nomura was valued by the stock market at over ¥11 trillion, or more than the stock markets of several countries. Making nearly $4 billion with just 12,000 employees was as incredible as it was certainly unsustainable. Another measure of Nomura's sheer financial muscle, and one the company has always regarded as a key gauge of its success, was the amount of cash and securities held in its clients' accounts. At the end of September 1989, near the peak of the Tokyo stock market, this figure totalled ¥61.2 trillion ($437 billion based on the then-current exchange rate of ¥140 to the dollar). This is the equivalent of 8 percent of America's GNP that year.

There are several reasons why Japan's top securities firms were so profitable and why they have managed to hang on to most of the profits they made during the boom years. First, unlike their stockbroking counterparts in London and New York they still, at least for now, enjoy fixed brokering commissions and so are not obliged to compete in a dog-eat-dog environment of deregulated rates. Second, the Big Four did not go on the same sort of hiring spree during the bull market as did their counterparts in London and New York. Nor do they pay their employees the seemingly absurd salaries common in those financial centers, which is why wages still only account for 35 percent of Nomura's expenses, compared with 70 percent of Merrill Lynch's, its closest American counterpart. The average Japanese retail salesman in a broker's branch office only earns a salary of about ¥8 million to ¥10 million a year, on top of which he might expect to receive a 20 percent bonus. This is peanuts by Wall Street standards.

The third and most important reason for the brokers' financial staying power is the way business is done. Thanks to fixed commissions Japanese brokers still act predominantly as agents rather than as principals. They do not have to commit their own capital to making markets in Japanese equities, which shields them from market risk. A similar 48 percent plunge in the stock market in London or New York, as occurred from peak to trough in Tokyo during 1990, would have resulted in huge trading losses for securities firms active in those markets. Japanese securities firms are also sensibly discouraged by finance ministry administrative guidance from making big bets for their own account, much less gambling huge chunks of their own capital on leveraged buyout deals as became commonplace in America in the late 1980s during Wall Street's craze for what became known, bizarrely, as "merchant banking." This self-restraint stems from controls introduced when Yamaichi, then Japan's biggest securities firm, nearly went bust in 1965 speculating with its own money and had to be rescued by the Bank of Japan. Consequently, Japanese securities firms own comparatively few shares for short-term investment purposes and so were much less badly hurt when the market crashed than were their major corporate clients, many of whom had become heavily involved in the 1980s fashion for *zaitech* (literally "financial engineering") where money seeking short-term gains was diverted from ordinary commercial use into the stock market via *tokkin* accounts. Nomura owned only ¥133 billion of equities in its trading account at the end of September 1991, an amount that represented less than 3 percent of its total assets. This low exposure to a falling stock market helped Nomura achieve net profits of ¥122.9 billion in the year ending March 1991. Although earnings collapsed further to ¥22 billion in the six months ending September 1991 in the wake of scandals, trading bans imposed on the firm, and further sharp declines in stock market trading volumes, it was remarkable that the firm was still making any money at all.

Nomura certainly has the financial resources to draw on. As a result of not frittering away the money it made in the boom years, Nomura is rock solid financially. The firm had shareholders' funds of ¥1.93 trillion at the end of March 1991, much of it deployed in liquid form. The interest income from this cash pile alone provides an important buttress in lean times. In the year ending March 1991 gross interest and income (including income made from extending margin loans to investors) accounted for ¥382 billion, or 39 percent of operating revenues, more than commission income, which contributed ¥318 billion, or 33 percent. Net interest income (after deducting all interest paid out) came to ¥142 billion. The same trend was even more pronounced in the six month period ending September 1991, when interest and dividend income reached ¥163 billion, compared with commission revenue of ¥114 billion.

Nomura's financial strength is also clear from the ease with which it meets the capital-adequacy standards set by the finance ministry for securities companies. These stipulate that stockbrokers must have enough liquid capital (defined broadly as shareholders' capital less fixed assets) to meet three months of operating costs, a 20 percent decline in the value of their securities holdings, and a 4 percent default rate in the margin loans they have extended to investors. Nomura's capital-adequacy ratio was 5.8 times this required minimum in September 1991. This means the firm could pay its operating expenses for three years without earning a single yen in revenue, a fabulously strong position.

Even though Nomura may well be the world's most humbled financial institution as a result of 1991's spate of summertime scandals and top-level resignations, its fall from grace is likely to prove strictly temporary precisely because its financial resources are so deep. It also helps that its response to adversity has been positive. The signs are that Nomura, formerly famous for its arrogance, has learned its lesson and made the smart but tough decision to transform the way it runs its equity business for the best practical reason: it no longer makes commercial sense. This is a brave move, since it means transforming the culture of the entire firm. But Nomura has the money, will, and know-how to effect such a change. It also has little choice if it wants to stay on top.

The firm's major competitors in Japan will have to follow Nomura's pioneering example if they are not to lag even farther behind. All the securities companies face a dual challenge of major proportions. They need to recast their corporate culture in the wake of the scandals while they prepare for what are likely to be sweeping changes in their industry. The two are connected. Prior to the scandals it seemed that the securities companies had successfully used their too-close connections with the Ministry of Finance—which, like all government ministries is located in Kasumigaseki, and which Tokyo wags described only half-jokingly as the Kasumigaseki branch of Nomura Securities—to fend off pressures to allow commercial banks into the securities business and to deregulate stockbroking commissions, as occurred after the Big Bang in London in 1986 and May Day in New York in 1974. The scandals put an end to those hopes by destroying the brokers' credibility. It is now generally accepted that if commissions had been set by the market in a competitive environment the securities firms would have been less profitable and so less inclined to pay compensation for losses to favored investors (of which more to come). Consequently, fixed commissions will within a few years be history in the Tokyo stock market. Nomura itself is preparing for that day. It estimates that by 1994 at the latest commissions will be negotiable for orders placed by institutional investors. That encounter with market forces will compel the securities companies to make radical changes, though at least they will have the precedents of London and New York to draw on. Small brokerage firms that are already losing money will be hard pressed to meet this challenge. Most of them will either fail or be forced into the arms of stronger competitors. The biggest firms should, after a few traumas, emerge stronger.

Nomura is likely to remain at the top. By the end of the 1980s the company was a superbly disciplined army known for its aggressive, highly centralized management and quasi-militaristic culture. But its very commercial success, and the institutional arrogance that increasingly went along with it, also succeeded in alienating large sections of Japan's traditional business establishment, from manufacturing companies to banks. Securities firms in Japan have always had the reputation for being engaged in a dirty, almost sleazy business; their employees are considered crooks at worst, parasitic intermediaries at best. Unlike their counterparts in London and New York, they have not traditionally been able to recruit the best graduates in Japan, though that began to change during the 1980s boom as the allure of Nomura's spectacular financial success, not to mention the glamour of its expanding overseas branches, attracted the best and brightest of graduates, to the growing resentment of other employers. Nonetheless, it remains true that in general, banks and upper-end manufacturers employ a far higher caliber of individual than do brokers in Japan.

Such traditional attitudes explain why upstart Nomura's humbling precipitated much naked glee and general Nomura bashing within Japan's industrial establishment. The Japanese press certainly gave Nomura a harder time than the other equally scandal-ridden brokerage firms. The scandals also reinforced many long-held popular stereotypes about the nature of the securities business and about the sort of people who are attracted to it.

Nomura's reaction to this abrupt fall from grace has been intelligent. Since the scandals (referred to in the long-delayed 1991 annual report as "recent incidents") senior management has been involved in what is officially described as a "discussion period," which still continues at the time of this writing. But the changes that will emerge from this process are already becoming clear. The initial results were announced at a September 20, 1991, meeting, which the heads of all 154 domestic branches and 63 foreign offices were summoned to attend. The most important change is the decision to grant autonomy to branch offices. Branches no longer receive daily instructions from the head office on what shares have to be sold and what sales quotas have to be met. The central sales office has been abolished, as have all sales targets. The branches are, as a consequence, left broadly to their own devices. This has created a vacuum that traditional Nomura types find bewildering; they now have no model to follow. But many younger employees consider the change positively liberating. An assistant manager at Nomura's biggest domestic branch in Tokyo's Shinjuku district is an example. He went to work in a domestic branch office in 1990 for the first time since joining Nomura in 1981 and after having spent more than seven years working for the firm overseas, first in Paris and later in London. Suddenly thrust back into the mainstream of Nomura's business, domestic retail brokering, he describes the postscandal atmosphere at the firm this way: "The people with low morality are doing nothing. Those with high morality are trying to change things." But he is well aware that morality alone is not enough to bring about the necessary changes. Nomura's retail brokers will have to learn the skills necessary for their new roles. Under the former centralized command system, a "good temperament" and "placing power" were all that were required of a Nomura man. In the future Nomura salesmen will have to display initiative and will have to have some grasp of the rudiments of economics to do their jobs properly, the assistant manager says. "Trust me" will no longer be enough.

Branch autonomy also means that for the first time in Nomura's history branches will not be evaluated on the amount of commission they generate but on whether they produce enough revenue to cover their overhead. This shift from pursuit of market share to managing costs could prove timely given the slump in the securities business and the need to budget in anticipation of the introduction of deregulated commissions. Tokyo stock market trading volume is way down and at the end of 1991 showed no sign of imminent recovery. The domestic underwriting business, the other key component of brokers' income, also remained depressed because of a continued finance ministry ban on domestic equity issues by listed companies. This ban was introduced in April 1990 as a way of reducing the supply of equity and so preventing a weak stock market from falling farther after its first slide. An attempt to get around this rule by floating a subsidiary backfired for Sony when it sought to list Sony Music Japan as a separate public company toward the end of 1991. The share issue underwritten by Nomura was priced too high and flopped badly. This served to deter many other companies that were hoping to do the same thing. They had been waiting to see how Sony, always somewhat of a corporate trendsetter, fared.

The second change proposed at Nomura is a new system for evaluating the firm's 12,500 employees in Japan. Evaluations will no longer be based almost solely on the amount of commission earned. The old Nomura workhorse salesman blindly following head office orders without an independent thought in his head is an endangered species. Nomura will increasingly want its salesmen to be qualified to advise retail clients how to manage their total financial portfolios, including shares, bonds, and cash. Senior management's model is Merrill Lynch, which is now as much a bank as it is a broker and has for several years awarded its retail brokers the grand-sounding title of "financial consultants." There has accordingly been much study within Nomura of how Merrill Lynch responded to Wall Street's October 1987 crash. As always, in adversity the Japanese are not too proud to learn from others.

Nomura will have to overcome regulatory obstacles in pursuit of this vision. A major stumbling block is that securities companies are not yet allowed to sell yen money-market funds in Japan. This is the product where Merrill Lynch scored its biggest bonanza in America. Its clients have had more than $100 billion deposited in money-market funds, which is why the firm can be likened accurately to a bank. The finance ministry may soon rule in favor of money-market funds in Japan, perhaps as a quid pro quo for allowing the banks to underwrite and deal in securities through specially created subsidiaries. Other areas full of promise for companies such as Nomura but again partially blocked by arcane regulations include the development of a liquid corporate bond market in Japan and the whole trend toward securitization. The latter is the process, long established in America, of pooling loans, be they mortgage loans, car loans, or even credit-card loans, and selling them off to investors as tradable asset-backed securities. The practice still barely exists in Japan.

Corporate bonds and securitization will develop because there is a pressing practical need for change on both fronts. With Japanese banks' loan growth so constrained by their dire lack of capital, such sorts of disintermediation must grow in Japan if only to make sure companies can obtain the financing they badly need. This will occur first through the development of a more liquid and active corporate bond market, and later by securitization. Nomura should be a prime beneficiary of both trends.

However, these developments will take time because there are so many cultural and regulatory obstacles to overcome. A domestic corporate bond market is a mainstay of finance in most developed economies. In Japan it has barely come of age. Corporate bond issues accounted for 47.5 percent of all corporate financing in America in 1989. In Japan the equivalent figure was just 2 percent, and nearly all of this was raised by utility companies operating with special privileges. This odd state of affairs is the result of quirky regulations and historical circumstance. Immediately after 1945 the government kept the bond market all to itself. Companies' long-term financing needs were instead funneled through the three long-term credit banks under the guiding hand of the then all-powerful MITI. That system gradually broke down as companies became less dependent on both official guidance and bank loans. Yet the anachronistic structure has remained in place to stifle development of a proper market serving companies' borrowing needs. One example of this outdated structure is the archaic commission bank system. Every domestic bond issue has a commission bank, which acts both as consultant to the issuer and as a trustee representing investors. The commission bank earns a fee for this compulsory service. This system gives banks control of the corporate bond market, even though securities houses actually launch the issues and do the underwriting. Since banks can look at every deal before it comes to market, they have traditionally kept the best credits for themselves by lending out the money directly. There are also strict limits on who can issue what. Only companies with an A credit rating can issue straight corporate bonds in Japan. This rule excludes more than two-thirds of the firms listed on the first and second sections of the Tokyo Stock Exchange. Would-be issuers must also contend with a lengthy queuing system. It can take up to three months to launch an issue. In the unregulated Euromarkets, by contrast, issues can be launched at a moment's notice.

An efficient corporate bond market in Japan would require at a minimum the following reforms. The archaic commission-banking system would have to go. In return banks would be allowed to underwrite and deal in corporate bonds. And the present underwriting and pricing cartel presided over by the Big Four securities firms would have to be abolished and replaced by a system where prices are set by the market. But even these reforms would not be enough. A change in mentality is also required because there remains in Japan scant awareness of the proper pricing of credit risk. The financial system still exhibits deep reluctance to mark assets to market, whether those assets are bank loans or shares owned by pension funds. Likewise, companies still tend to borrow from banks at the same percentage over the prime rate regardless of their business prospects and of how much money they owe. The absence of a liquid corporate bond market also means Japan lacks any equivalent to America's yield spreads that reflect credit risk through the number of extra basis points (hundredths of a percentage point) that a corporate bond yields over American Treasury bonds. Still there are now finally signs of progress in this area prompted by companies' increasingly pressing financing needs. Japanese companies raised some ¥6 trillion in corporate bond issues in 1991. This is not bad considering there were only ¥8.9 trillion in domestic corporate bonds outstanding in March 1990. The total for 1992 is likely to be higher still. There are also problems with developing securitization in Japan because, as with corporate bonds, it raises a thorny turf issue: whether banks, as well as stockbrokers, can deal in asset-backed securities. This problem has so far delayed a final decision on this issue even though the banks badly need to shrink their assets (by securitizing them and selling them off) and so boost their capital. There is also a cultural difficulty with securitization in Japan; it demands far more transparency than Japanese borrowers and lenders are used to or comfortable with. Investors interested in buying these securities will want access to all sorts of data, such as default rates. These can be hard to obtain in murky Japan, which is why securitization will probably take longer to develop than a liquid corporate bond.

The new-look Nomura should also mean radical changes in institutional equity brokering in Japan since the firm's competition will seek to emulate its example. Nomura will upgrade its second-rate brokering research effort by tapping the resources of its own more respected Nomura Research Institute. This is critical, since the firm's intellectual credibility is at stake. Nomura, like other Japanese brokers, was made to look foolish and useless by its failure to warn, let alone prepare, clients for Tokyo's crash in 1990, and by its failure to alter its bullish stance during the course of that crash. Investment managers were not impressed and were taught a valuable lesson about the value of independent research. This is why foreign brokers' market share of the Tokyo Stock Exchange's shrunken commission business had risen from 3 percent in 1989 to 15 percent by the end of 1991. Insider tips and share promotions, the traditional hallmarks of Japanese stockbroking, are not much use in a bear market. Being stubbornly bullish on everything to do with Japan is now a habit of the past, as out of date as blatant share ramps, compensating favored clients for losses, and consorting with gangsters.

The extent to which Japan's professional investors are disillusioned with their own securities firms should not be underestimated. Stockbrokers in recent years had become increasingly out of tune with their Japanese fund-manager clients, because they had failed to notice their clients had become more savvy about investing. They were growing more demanding about the type of brokering service they received, as they learned more about investing overseas and gained more exposure to the services offered by foreign stockbrokers. When Japanese stock prices started falling, Japanese institutional investors, such as life insurers and trust banks, turned increasingly in their hour of need to foreign securities firms, especially Morgan Stanley and Salomon Brothers, to hedge their huge share portfolios through the selling of stock index futures. This was a brand new market, since stock index futures only began to be traded in Japan in 1988. But their existence meant Japanese investors were now able to hedge their huge share portfolios without having to disrupt commercial relationships by selling their long-term cross-shareholdings. The foreign securities firms' success in these new markets naturally upset local brokers. They are uncomfortable with, if not plain ignorant of, the derivative techniques associated with the world of futures and options, the investment business's equivalent of high technology. Yet after several months of blaming, quite absurdly, this sort of index arbitrage (more commonly though misleadingly known as program trading) for the stock market's woes the Big Four increasingly stopped moaning and started copying, with varying though limited degrees of success. Their problem is that they are still comparative novices in Wall Street–pioneered computerized-trading techniques. The finance ministry and the Tokyo Stock Exchange also made a series of ridiculous moves during 1990 to try to make arbitrage more difficult, the effect of which was only to make the futures market more illiquid and therefore more dangerously volatile should investors panic and rush to sell simultaneously. This was not the sort of interference designed to inspire confidence in a wobbly market.

By 1991 there were signs that an attempt was being made to use stock index futures to support the market. Stock index futures were consistently overvalued relative to shares for the whole of that year. The result was a perilous situation that gave a few sleepless nights to those invested heavily in Japanese shares. The

best explanation for the constant premium is that Japanese investors had decided that futures provided the cheapest way to buy
shares, or at least of maintaining an exposure to the stock market
while tying up as little cash as possible. This makes sense. Commissions in the futures market are one-tenth those in the stock
market, and brokers who buy futures only have to put up 8 percent
in cash and 17 percent in shares of the value of each contract. The
rest of the money is free to earn interest on deposit. The snag was
that the resulting overvaluation of futures compared with shares
caused by this constant premium created a grand opportunity for
index arbitrageurs, the biggest of whom in Tokyo are Salomon and
Morgan Stanley. They pocketed that premium by selling overvalued futures and buying undervalued shares, as did many other
foreign securities firms, though on a smaller scale. The result has
been a record overhang of arbitrage-related buying of stock index
futures (overhang being the amount of futures that have to be
bought back or rolled over to the next futures contract before expiry
of existing futures contract), which toward the end of 1991 peaked
at around ¥1.5 trillion worth of shares. This overhang is dangerous. If a sudden piece of news should turn everyone bearish simultaneously (an earthquake, perhaps) it could precipitate a downward
plunge as arbitrage positions, instead of being rolled over to the
new contract as the old expire, are suddenly unwound, so that
futures are bought and shares sold, pushing the futures to a discount. Then selling of shares could prompt unhedged futures investors to sell, which would again push the futures to a discount,
which in turn would trigger more program selling of shares, and so
on.

A further worry is that not everyone will be able to get through
the door as it slams shut. This is no idle fear. In theory, abritrage
should make markets more efficient by bringing futures and cash
prices into line. But in Tokyo, regulators have introduced absurdly
narrow limits on how far futures contracts can move without a
trading halt being called. Trading is suspended for six minutes each
time the Nikkei index moves by thirty points, a tiny amount. It is
not uncommon for the futures markets to spend most of the day

not trading, leaving the stock market with no benchmark against which to fluctuate. The reduced volume of stock market trading makes matters still more treacherous. The number of shares represented by ¥1.5 trillion of outstanding futures contracts is several times the number of shares that were being traded daily in the stock market at the end of 1991. Yet to unwind the arbitrage means selling that amount of shares.

Investors are well aware of this problem, as are the authorities, though there is a risk that they will become too aware and complacency will set in. Nerves become frayed whenever the futures contract is close to its expiration or whenever the stock market falls to near 20,000 on the Nikkei. In June 1991, for example, several foreign securities firms active in index arbitrage were summoned to the Tokyo Stock Exchange. The ostensible purpose of these meetings, backed up by "informal" telephone calls from the finance ministry, was to gather information on outstanding arbitrage positions. The real point was to find out what premium would be required on the September futures contract to make sure the arbitrage positions were rolled over prior to the expiration of the June contract. The authorities got the information they were looking for. During the week before the June contract expired, buying of the September contract by Japanese brokers pushed the premium on the futures up from 620 Nikkei points to 700, even though the stock market was falling during that period. In effect, index arbitrageurs (mostly foreign brokers) were handed a blank check, or a "ransom" as some of them called it, to entice them to roll over—and so they did. This extra yield gave them an annualized yield of over ten percentage points on their arbitrage positions, net of all borrowing costs, a handsome return on capital in what is essentially a riskless trade. On Wall Street program traders would be happy to make a one-percentage-point return in the same sort of business. This is the main reason why Morgan Stanley and Salomon made more money than Nikko in the first half of the 1991 fiscal year. During this time, each foreign firm made about ¥20 billion from trading their own capital, according to figures they submitted to the Tokyo Stock Exchange. Most of this came from such index arbitrage. As the arbitrageurs' profits grow, and other foreign firms increasingly allocate more capital to this same activity, the resulting overhang will get bigger as does the risk that it will one day unwind unpleasantly. However, the overhang would disappear if Japanese investors would stop paying such a steep premium for the futures. The main culprits are the investment trusts, the equivalent of America's mutual funds and Britain's unit trusts. They have bought futures because they have to be exposed to the stock market but they want to tie up as little cash as possible to meet anticipated redemptions. At the beginning of 1992 there were signs that the investment trusts were beginning to wake up to the self-defeating nature of this exercise as a result of the losses they were taking on their futures positions. By buying futures at a big premium they were simply handing profits to foreign arbitrageurs and exposing themselves to a loss. In a zero-sum game like futures, there has to be a loser for every winner.

Index arbitrage is the high-tech end of the securities business. At a more mundane but equally critical level, Japanese securities firms' task is to try to hang on to as many of their disillusioned private clients as possible. It will not be easy. In recognition of the obvious they have stopped concentrating on selling speculative shares and are instead stressing more boringly sensible strategies like selling government bonds to a concerned public, just as Wall Street firms did after the October 1987 crash. One major problem Japanese firms face is that their large retail branch networks could rapidly become expensive fixed costs in a slow market if the sales network is no longer exploited in the traditional ruthlessly efficient manner whereby sales campaigns are centralized, every branch has a quota to meet, and every salesman is pushing the same shares. This is the risk in Nomura's decision to change its modus operandi. By granting branches autonomy it has consciously backed away from what made the company such a formidable sales machine in the first place.

The last time Japan suffered a proper sort of three-year-long bear market was in the mid-1960s when Yamaichi nearly failed. At that time the number of employees in the securities industry fell from 100,000 to 60,000. This time it could be worse. There are now about 150,000 people working in the business, of whom at least 50,000 do not have the knowledge and sophistication to handle a deregulated financial world where they have to come up with their own ideas and not simply obey head office orders.

Japanese securities firms will also have to change their attitude toward smaller private clients, whom they have tended to treat badly, a habit they got away with only because of the stock market's extraordinary performance. Between 1970 and 1989 the stock market rose nearly 2,000 percent. This performance covered up a multitude of brokers' sins. Take for example the securities firms' appalling record of managing investment trusts, the retail vehicles they tended to dump shares into at the tail end of a share ramp after the important institutional clients had sold out. Thus the investment trusts (which tend to be 50 percent invested in equities) achieved an annual return of only 4 percent during the 1980s, compared with the Nikkei index's 21 percent annual rate of return, according to an estimate by the securities firm Jardine Fleming. The investment trusts came in handy for the brokers. They were the ideal vehicle for generating commissions because the securities company controlled both the brokering and the investing. The trusts were also used to help prop up the market. Most investment trusts set up during the bull market locked investors in for a fixed period, usually two years. Managers of these funds did not have to worry about a wave of investors asking for their money back, as they tend to do when markets fall. Between 1986 and 1989 the investment trust companies sold ¥53 trillion of these funds. About half of this money was invested in shares, providing powerful fuel to the roaring market.

A glimpse of how Japanese brokers operate and how shoddily they can treat private clients is provided by an action brought in November 1989 and still bogged down in Japan's tortuously slow legal system. Suit was brought by Wakabayashi Real Estate against New Japan Securities, Japan's fifth-largest securities firm. New Japan is linked to (but, by law, not more than 5 percent owned by) Industrial Bank of Japan. The case concerns two accounts set up by

Koji Wakabayashi, president of the property company that he inherited from his father in 1986 at the age of thirty-six. An account at New Japan was set up in August 1987 from the proceeds of property sales. The money was initially invested in medium-term government bonds. The aim was to keep the funds relatively liquid with a view to reinvesting the money in property.

But the eager beavers at New Japan evidently had other ideas. Two of its employees regularly visited Wakabayashi, urging him to invest in shares; one employee was from New Japan's Tokyo head office, the other from its branch in Omori, the Tokyo district where Wakabayashi had his office. Wakabayashi, who claims he had no experience in securities matters, was at first reluctant to take this advice since he wanted to keep the funds liquid. New Japan told him that this was not an obstacle because it could arrange a loan using his company's bond holdings as collateral. Thus comforted, Wakabayashi set up two trading accounts in his company's name, both of the margin type, at New Japan's head office and its Omori branch. (A margin account allows an investor to borrow up to twice the value of the funds in the account for the purpose of buying shares.) He claims no one at New Japan warned him, orally or in writing, of the risks associated with margin trading.

The Wakabayashi Real Estate accounts proceeded to be turned over at a frantic rate. Between September 1987 and January 1989, 1,163 trades were executed in the two accounts. The transactions totaled ¥13.9 billion. This was lucrative business for the broker. New Japan earned ¥185.5 million in commissions and another ¥21.8 million in margin interest during this period. Turnover was hectic. On average a given stock was held for less than twenty-one days, and none was held for more than one year. Approximately 46 percent of all shares bought were held for less than one week. The unfortunate result was that, though the Tokyo stock market was going up during this period, the two accounts ended up showing a net loss of ¥122.8 million, primarily because of all that commission money paid to New Japan.

This looks like a classic instance of churning, but the weakness in Wakabayashi Real Estate's case is that these were not discretionary accounts, for which the broker could initiate transactions without obtaining the client's permission. Still, Wakabayashi's lawyers argue that New Japan had de facto control of the accounts since buy and sell orders were only initiated as a result of recommendations from the broker. Wakabayashi even claims that sometimes he did not receive confirmation of a share sale before another share had been bought with the sale's proceeds. Whatever the legal outcome of this case, it does give a hint of why Japanese brokers suffer from such a bad name.

Still, this reputation did not deter most of corporate Japan from piling into the stock market to play the *zaitech* game during the bubble years. For Japanese brokers not only had less direct exposure to the stock market than banks or life insurers, but also less than many nonfinancial companies as well. The stock market crash drove a hole through the profits of the many Japanese companies that had become used to boosting their earnings through short-term gambling in *tokkin* funds. Such *zaitech* profits accounted for 15 percent of the earnings reported in 1989 by companies listed on the Tokyo Stock Exchange.

But this is small potatoes compared with another longer-term effect the stock market crash will have on companies' finances. Low interest rates and rising stock prices also enabled Japanese companies to borrow lots of money almost for free in the 1980s through equity-linked financing, be it bonds with warrants attached or covertible bonds. In fiscal 1989, for example, ¥18.5 trillion of warrants and convertible bonds was issued. This was an underwriting bonanza for the securities firms, and provided corporate Japan with an attractive substitute for a domestic corporate bond market. The center of the action was London's Euromarkets, where Nomura rose to the top of the underwriting tables by creating a Japanese market away from home. The issuers of the paper were Japanese, as were most of the buyers.

The warrant phenomenon is noteworthy not only because of the amount of cheap money it raised but also because of the resulting supply of potentially worthless paper it created, which now hangs over the stock market like a lead balloon and which has the consequent refinancing implications for corporate Japan. As such, it is one of the bills still left to be paid from the bursting of the Bubble Economy.

Financial instruments that claim to keep everybody happy usually end up making most people miserable. Warrants are a classic case. During the 1980s the favorite financial fix of many Japanese firms came from equity warrants, which seemed to offer almost limitless supplies of cheap capital. The warrants were issued with bonds that usually had a maturity of five years. The warrant gave the right during the bond's life to buy new shares in the issuing company at 5 percent above the price on a particular date, the so-called "exercise" price. In return for this perk the bond carried a very low yield.

Between 1987 and 1989 Japanese companies issued some $115 billion of bonds with warrants attached. The total outstanding is now around $170 billion. Nearly all these securities were issued in dollars. In theory, everybody won. Many warrants quadrupled or more in price as the stock market soared. And, thanks to Japan's supereasy monetary policy and the intricacies of the international swap markets, companies enjoyed incredibly favorable financing terms. The dollar bonds usually carried coupons as low as 1 to 3 percent, but borrowing turned out even cheaper than that because by the time the Japanese borrowing companies swapped their dollar exposure into yen (whose interest rate was then as much as five percentage points lower than the dollar's) their cost of capital turned negative. In other words, they were paid to borrow.

Japanese borrowers have tended to view warrants they issue as money in the bank. But if warrants never come into the money because the company's stock price never reaches the price at which the warrants can be converted into equity, then investors will not exercise the warrants by buying new shares, and those proceeds will not be available to repay the bondholders when the bonds mature.

This is exactly what is likely to happen thanks to the protracted slump in the Tokyo stock market. The warrants will turn around and bite the hands of those who issued them. That will force the issuers of these instruments to refinance the bonds at what will likely be much higher interest rates. Baring Securities estimates that Japanese companies may have to repay nearly $170 billion they never thought they would have to when the bulk of these warrants expire between 1991 and 1994. (They may also have to repay another $200 billion of convertible bonds that mature unconverted, though most of them do not mature until 1994 or later.) Warrants are also a nuisance for the stock market. The threat of all those warrants waiting to be converted is a major supply constraint undermining any prospect of a sustained rally in the stock market. There are, for example, an estimated ¥7 trillion of warrants and convertible bonds waiting to be converted between 27,000 and 30,000 on the Nikkei index. For this very reason the Tokyo stock market will encounter stiff resistance any time it begins to approach those levels. The rally in March 1991 petered out at 27,000, the rally in October 1991 at 25,000. This is one reason why the Nikkei ended 1991 slightly below where it began the year despite ¥5.6 trillion of net purchases of Japanese shares by foreign investors that year and despite steep falls in long-term and short-term interest rates as Japan's bond market soared, in response to a slowing economy, and as the Bank of Japan eased monetary policy amid growing confirmation that the economy was indeed slowing faster than official forecasts anticipated and the central bank was officially prepared to admit. The foreigners' mistake was to conclude prematurely that the crash of 1990 represented a bargain. In fact, the concept of a bargain was relative. The market was still not cheap; it was just less expensive. In early 1992 shares were still trading on a price-earnings ratio of 40 times companies' forecasted earnings and yielding only 0.8 percent, even though the Nikkei index was back flirting with the 20,000 bottom reached in October 1990, which was far below the level required to enable most of the warrants to be converted.

By this time panic was beginning to set in among the brokers. The bear market had simply lasted too long. The shock of losing money was being replaced by mounting desperation, and a nagging worry that things would never get better again. A mood of futile nostalgia began to pervade financial circles in Tokyo, a yearning for the golden days when stock prices could be supported by administrative decree or rank manipulation. On January 23, 1992, the Big Four securities firms held a widely publicized Tuesday-morning breakfast meeting to decide what to do about the sick stock market. These breakfast meetings had become part of Tokyo bull market mythology, the occasions when the brokers were supposed to decide which shares each firm would push to avoid unnecessary competition. The January 23 meeting was billed as the first such gathering since the previous summer's scandals. But on this occasion the assembled stockbrokers could think of nothing better to do than set up a working party and float senseless ideas like market-support funds. Just such a government-sponsored stabilization fund had worked to rally the market in 1965, but on that occasion the stock market was very cheap and the banks had plenty of spare capital to invest in shares. Neither circumstance was true in 1992. The much-heralded meeting proved a comedown from the Big Four's triumphant Tuesday-morning meetings during the bull market.

The finance ministry was equally bereft of ideas on how to revive the stock market. It could call in the Big Four and order them to buy, as it had in the old days, but they would probably no longer obey. As a consequence of the scandals, relations were too strained, especially with Nomura, and confidence too shattered for such tactics to work. In desperation, finance ministry officials began threatening to clamp down on futures trading. There was even vague talk of imposing quotas on the arbitrage activities of foreign securities firms, a message that was conveyed not so vaguely to the firms in question. Such measures would probably have been introduced had it not been for fear of further inflaming trade tensions with America. The two biggest arbitrage firms, Morgan Stanley and Salomon Brothers, were, of course, American houses. Doubtless with finance ministry approval, the Tokyo Stock Exchange announced it would set up a task force to study futures trading. This move was made in response to growing pressures from its Japanese member securities firms, most of whom had scant understanding of the world of futures and options and who were fond of blaming a combination of foreigners and futures for their problems. Ironically, it was buying by foreigners—fund managers, not brokers—that had saved Japan's stock market, and therefore its banks and its financial system, from suffering an even worse implosion during 1991. Meanwhile, expectations were that should the Nikkei index fall below 20,000, a package of market-support measures would be sure to emerge, however ineffective. This was the level official Japan had chosen to defend.

These were the big issues at stake in the Tokyo bear market. They went far beyond the narrow world of the stock market. But the stock market's collapse exposed scandals and provided a revealing glimpse of the seedy underbelly of Japanese finance. The subsequent exposure and humiliation served as a useful catalyst for those securities firms ready to accept the challenge and make changes that were long overdue. The bear market would eventually have compelled Japanese stockbrokers to change their approach to business anyway. But there is nothing like a good scandal to force the issue.

# 6

# Brokering Scandals

It was September 1991. The scene was the Liberal Democratic Party headquarters in Tokyo's Nagatacho district, right next to the Japanese Diet. The occasion was a meeting between selected heads of foreign securities firms and the LDP committee responsible for financial reform.

The foreigners' hopeless mission in arranging this meeting was to try to prevent the securities scandals causing deregulation of Japanese stockbroking commissions, a change that would affect them as adversely as it would Japanese securities firms. But in making their pitch to the politicians they could not avoid addressing the controversial events of that summer. James Walsh, president of America's Prudential Securities in Japan, came up with a useful analogy in his presentation. It ran as follows: An athlete wants to bulk up his muscles but for competitive reasons cannot afford the time to achieve this through daily training. So he begins taking anabolic steroids regularly with the result that he becomes bigger and faster than his competitors. He takes the drug over an extended period of time, so the short-term impact is not obvious. But after a while his organs begin to malfunction, a tumor appears, and comprehensive physical deterioration ensues at a much faster pace than his initial buildup. The athlete dies.

Mr. Walsh noted that "It is crucial to understand that the

practice of reimbursing certain investors for their losses in the Japanese securities market was in fact the equivalent of a steroid treatment that has debilitated the market process in Japan. These were not 'emergency' measures undertaken in the face of a significant market drop for a one-time repair. They were not compelled to assure the survival of clients. Neither were they enhancements to otherwise weakened investors, unable to bear the cost of realizing their investment losses. Rather it was a practice to manipulate regularly the market by replacing losses for certain investors.''

The steroid analogy is useful. The practice of compensating important investors for their losses was ultimately counterproductive because it undermined the raison d'être of stockbroking. This is now understood by the younger talent inside Nomura. Take the branch manager of Nomura's office in the Shimbashi district of Tokyo. He returned to Japan at the end of 1989 to assume his current post after spending more than nine years working overseas in Frankfurt and London. The branch manager is a thoughtful person. He understands the key point about equity investment that had clearly eluded or at least been forgotten by some of his former bosses and that should be taught to every newcomer to the securities business. This fact is that equities represent the risk capital of the world. Nomura's business, defined at its most basic level, is the handling of that risk capital. To pretend that risk does not exist is therefore to make a nonsense of the art (certainly not the science) of stockbroking. He says, "If we deny risk our business cannot be done. This compensation business is a nonsense for all our business." These are strong words for a Japanese stockbroker, even though they were uttered after the scandal. They also make a lot of sense.

However self-defeating it may have been, the loss-compensation scandal needs to be put in a chronological context since it had its origins in long-established practices. It was a typically Japanese saga where conspiracy has been mistaken for confusion. The specific issue of how to deal with loss-compensation practices in the Japanese stock market actually had its origins in two finance ministry directives issued to the securities companies two days before the Nikkei index reached its all-time high on the last day of 1989. The first directive instructed brokers to end *eigyo tokkin* accounts immediately. The *eigyo tokkin* were a special sort of *tokkin* account where the securities firms themselves, rather than investment advisory firms, managed the money. Some ¥4 trillion was invested in such accounts. The securities firms encouraged companies to set up these *eigyo tokkin* by offering them guaranteed returns. This explains the finance ministry's second directive, which banned such compensation of investors' losses. This would seem to suggest that if there were losses on the *eigyo tokkin* investors could not have them made good. Four months later, in March 1990, the losses were suddenly no longer theoretical. The stock market had by then already embarked upon its steep descent, and many investors in *eigyo tokkin* were already under water. This made the finance ministry's two directives, seeking to ban both *eigyo tokkin* and loss compensation, appear both contradictory and impractical to the securities firms, for it was hard to wind down those accounts in an orderly fashion without paying those guarantees. At this point, according to insiders in Nomura, the finance ministry told the securities firms (in what if true amounted to a classic example of verbal "administrative guidance") that the priority should be placed on closing down the *eigyo tokkin.* The quickest way to do this without protracted disputes was obviously to honor the guarantees. So, it is alleged, officials effectively turned a blind eye to loss compensation.

This version of events explains Nomura's subsequent fury at the way the scandal erupted. The catalyst, as with so many scandals in history, was the tax man. The tax authorities blew the whistle on the affair and leaked the details to the press to thwart finance ministry efforts at a cover-up. This may seem odd since the tax bureau, the nearest equivalent to America's Internal Revenue Service or Britain's Inland Revenue, is formally incorporated within the finance ministry. In practice, however, the tax bureau is independent in both spirit and action.

The irony is that loss compensation only became a tax matter because the securities firms tried cheekily to deduct their compen-

sation payments by declaring them as business payments. The tax
inspectors would have none of this. They ruled instead that they
were entertainment expenses, which are not deductible. The first
tax cases concerning this practice were actually brought in 1989
when Daiwa, Yamaichi, and eighteen other securities firms owned
up to making compensation payments totaling ¥18 billion and
were fined accordingly. This scandal died a comparatively quick
death. But these cases prompted the finance ministry to issue its
guideline at the end of 1989. At that time Nomura denied that it
was engaged in the practice. Few believed this. By the time it came
to Nomura and Nikko's turn in June 1990 to own up to the
practice, loss compensation had suddenly become an altogether
more controversial affair. This was in part because of a separate
scandal involving these same two securities firms' business dealings with gangsters (of which more later). But in the wake of the
stock market crash it also reflected increased public outrage at the
revelation that big fish were being bailed out while the small-fry
were expected to suffer their losses without complaining. Even
though it has long been common knowledge within Tokyo's financial community that Japanese securities firms did make good
favored investors' losses, the disclosure came as an undoubted
shock to many ordinary folk. Their response was genuine indigna-
tion. Hence the need for public sacrifices. On June 24, Yoshihisa
("Little") Tabuchi, president of mighty Nomura, and Takuya
Iwasaki, president of Nikko, Japan's third-largest securities firm,
resigned. Although both men were moved upstairs to vice-chair-
manships, their public humiliation was real. The overly optimistic
hope at the time was that this sacrifice of big shots would mark
*kejime*, the point at which a line is drawn, a public sacrifice is
offered, and past transgressions are forgiven. The public would be
appeased and the scandal would be at an end. This was not so
unreasonable a hope, especially as no crime seemed to be involved.
It was legal to pay compensation in Japan, though to promise to do
so was not.

If members of the financial community, Japanese or foreign,
were not shocked by the details of the transgressions, they were

surprised that these matters were suddenly considered worthy of public revelation. From this soon developed a conspiracy theory. The guaranteeing of investment returns had indeed become an endemic feature of Japan's domestic fund-management industry in the previous fifteen years, and it was seen as a necessary tool for winning business. Not uncoincidentally, this practice became established during a period when stock prices were generally rising. The potential financial liability of the guarantor was therefore considered largely academic, because until 1990 the Tokyo stock market kept going up. The Big Four securities firms at the time of Little Tabuchi's resignation had owned up to paying a total of ¥65 billion between 1988 and March 1990 to compensate mostly corporate clients for their losses (more admissions were to follow later). These payments concerned just *eigyo tokkin* accounts. But *eigyo tokkin* was only the most flagrant example of guaranteeing investment returns, a practice that is so much a part of the investment business in Japan that it touches virtually every activity, from trust banks managing pension funds to stockbrokers' verbal agreements with individual clients. Clearly such widespread manipulation helped push the stock market to its ridiculous levels in the late 1980s, since investors were that much more eager to invest if they thought their risk of loss was underwritten. The funds thus informally guaranteed were probably so vast that Peter Tasker, a respected Tokyo-based investment strategist at Kleinwort, Benson, a British merchant bank, was prompted to comment in his weekly column that "the money to fill in that little hole simply does not exist."

There is a natural temptation, especially among some more conspiratorially inclined foreigners, to suggest a more Machiavellian interpretation for why this practice was suddenly considered worthy of public exposure. It is suggested that the loss-compensation scandal was a stage-managed affair, a spectacle designed to let the securities firms off the financial hook of having to honor their guarantees. According to this theory, Tabuchi and Iwasaki were ordered to resign by the finance ministry because it had become clear that the brokers could not meet their obligations. This seems too clever by half. First, the way the scandal oozed out via the tax inspectors did not look the slightest bit orchestrated. For example, Nomura initially denied the allegations after the first exclusive article appeared in the *Yomiuri Shimbun*, Japan's biggest general-circulation daily newspaper. Second, the long-overrated mandarins from the finance ministry emerged from the affair almost as big losers as the brokers, who had much less of a reputation to lose in the first place. There was, for example, a high-placed private scolding of the bureaucracy, word of which soon echoed around Japan's tight-knit business and political establishment. The top civil servant in the finance ministry, Horishi Yasuda, as well as the heads of its banking and securities bureaus, Masaaki Tsuchida and Nobuhiko Matsuno, were summoned to the prime minister's office on June 26. Toshiki Kaifu, then prime minister, told them to put their house in order and not to count on *amakudari*, literally, a "descent from heaven." *Amakudari* is the cozy practice whereby after retirement, senior bureaucrats go to work for the firms they have spent a career regulating. For finance ministry officials that has usually meant banks and securities companies. The finance ministry also had to withstand a great deal of public rebuke, a form of chastisement it was not at all used to and that damaged its hitherto august reputation both within the bureaucracy and throughout the country. There were countless editorials in both the domestic and foreign press arguing that Japan needed an independent securities regulator akin to America's Securities and Exchange Commission. The criticisms were so vocal because it was widely, and correctly, assumed that the finance ministry had known about the compensation arrangements on the *eigyo tokkin* for some time.

The final reason why it seems clear the scandal was not orchestrated was the extraordinary public outburst by Nomura's departing president. Little Tabuchi did not play his appointed part. Rather than fall silently on his symbolic sword, a clearly furious Tabuchi told shareholders at Nomura's annual general meeting that the finance ministry had not only approved the payments made by Nomura to favored clients to compensate them for their investment losses, but it had also given the firm the green light to deduct those payments against taxes. The former Nomura president's charge of finance ministry collusion may have come as no surprise to Tokyo moneymen. But that is not the point. The expression of that charge in public certainly was a complete shock. In fact no one could remember anything quite like it. For it is not permissible in Japan for the Ministry of Finance to admit to wrongdoing, and certainly no one in the financial community, Japanese or foreign, ever dares openly criticize it. The prevailing attitude, with the honorable exception of one or two leading Wall Street firms, has tended to be fawning deference.

The official response to Little Tabuchi's outburst was retaliation. The finance ministry announced it would ban Nomura and Nikko from securities dealing for a period later that year, a threat on which it subsequently acted. In a further indication of establishment anger with Nomura, its chairman, Setsuya "Big" Tabuchi (no relation to the departed president), was dismissed from his position as vice-chairman of the Keidanren, Japan's powerful Federation of Economic Organizations, big business's premier lobbying group. He had already offered to resign, but the Keidanren chairman, Gaishi Hiraiwa, spoiled the effect by stating publicly that Tabuchi would have been removed anyway.

Nomura had some right to be upset about its treatment at the hands of the finance ministry, for the bureaucrats essentially changed the rules halfway through the game. The Nomura view is that the finance minister at the time, Ryutaro Hashimoto, panicked in face of the public outcry when he himself described the payments as "compensation," thereby conceding the principle that such payments were indeed a bad thing. Nomura insiders argue that these payments could have been portrayed as legitimate business expenses required to wind up the *eigyo tokkin* in line with the finance ministry's wishes. This point is debatable. But what is not in doubt is that by paying compensation Nomura probably thought it was doing the right thing, that its action was justified because it was supporting the level of the stock market. As indeed it was, but for this compensation investors would have been that much more likely to liquidate their *eigyo tokkin* accounts earlier, causing some ¥3 trillion of selling pressure in an already weak stock market. That is also why the finance ministry's pragmatic instincts led its officials to turn a blind eye when the securities firms ignored its directive at a time when the ministry had no desire to exacerbate the stock market's decline.

This way of thinking draws attention to the uncomfortably close working relationship that existed between the finance ministry and the leading securities companies prior to the scandals. Part of the reason for this almost incestuous network lay in the official desire to ensure support for the market whenever there was a whiff of panic about. For example, the finance ministry called in the Big Four and ordered them to buy shares during the October 1987 crash and again in October 1990 when the Nikkei fell briefly below 20,000. On both occasions these actions were hailed throughout the world's financial community as a sign that Japan had a market-support mechanism that worked, in stark contrast to the seeming chaos that at times seems to prevail in more free-market environments like New York and Hong Kong. Indeed, in 1987 the finance ministry was hailed by many who should have known better as the savior of world capitalism. But there has always been a problem with such official intervention. By its very actions, the finance ministry itself encouraged a manipulative attitude toward markets. It also created a problem of moral hazard since the brokers acted on the assumption that they were underwritten against market risk because they were doing the bureaucracy's bidding. This state of affairs is now history. The sense of trust and communality of interest no longer exists between Nomura and the finance ministry, and it will be hard to rebuild them. The next time the Tokyo stock market crashes Nomura may not be so willing to do what the finance ministry tells it to. So another of the traditional props that investors happily took advantage of when they bought Japanese shares—namely the institutional mechanisms in place for supporting the market—can no longer be taken for granted. This is one of the important consequences of the loss-compensation scandal. The Japanese stock market will be healthier for it in the long run. But it will be a riskier place to invest money.

For a scandal that many alleged to have been an orchestrated affair, the loss-compensation saga certainly ran on and on. The securities firms kept owning up to having paid more compensation than they had earlier confessed to, and further acts of public atonement were consequently demanded of them. On July 22, 1991, Big Tabuchi himself resigned. This was a surprise, since this outwardly avuncular figure had been expected to ride out the furor on the argument that he had not been responsible for day-to-day business. But Big Tabuchi, who had spent much of his chairmanship cultivating senior political figures in a failed bid to get Nomura accepted by the establishment, was evidently given the word from lofty political circles that it was time for him to bow out. On the same day, Little Tabuchi resigned as vice-chairman, only a month after he had stepped down as president. But the penance was not that great. Both Tabuchis stayed on as advisers to Nomura, complete with their own offices at the firm's Tokyo head office, and both continued to draw salaries. Contrast that with the treatment meted out to former Salomon Brothers chairman John Gutfreund, who was forced to resign only a few weeks later for not having disclosed internal evidence of his firm's manipulation of American Treasury bond auctions. Gutfreund had worked for Salomon for thirty-eight years, yet he was suddenly forced to fend for himself, obliged to pay for his own office, secretaries, and lawyers in any action the federal government might choose to bring against him.

Big Tabuchi's resignation marked a watershed for Nomura, for there was no strongman, groomed for leadership, ready to replace him. This was shown in the choice of his quasi-successor as "honorary" chairman. He was Yukio Aida, an almost schoolmasterly figure far removed from the rough and tumble of domestic stockbroking who had spent twenty years dealing with international affairs at Nomura and who was summoned to his new position out of retirement. Aida was the ideal choice as the acceptable public face of Nomura, giving press interviews designed to restore the firm's battered image, and he spent most of his time doing just that in the next few months. But his distance from the firm's political power base and real decision-making was painfully apparent from the fact that he preferred to work from his old office in the Nomura Research Institute, the company's think tank.

Aida's arrival coincided with fresh estimates of the amount of compensation Japanese firms had paid. The Big Four now said they had paid 231 mostly corporate investors almost $1 billion between March 1987 and March 1990. This represented most of the ¥172 billion that Japan's seventeen largest securities firms had by then owned up to paying in compensation. One reason why the estimates kept changing is that loss compensation was not quite as crude a matter as it was usually depicted in the press. It did not, for example, usually take the form of handing over Ivan Boesky–style briefcases filled with cash. The techniques employed were rather more complex. One favorite ruse was buying back warrants at inflated prices. Another more subtle method took the form of dealing in government bonds with favored clients at slightly above or below prevailing market prices.

A report released by Japan's Securities Dealers Association in August 1990 found that 93 percent of all reimbursed losses were made through sales and purchases of bonds with warrants, or ¥160.3 billion of the total ¥172 billion owned up to. By contrast, compensating for losses through the allocation of newly issued shares only totaled ¥4.1 billion. The actual mechanics of arranging warrant compensation could be highly complex, involving shifting funds around the globe in a convoluted series of transactions. Tax inspectors described how Nomura disguised ¥4.5 billion of compensation paid to Showa Shell Sekiyu, a major oil refiner, and others following the October 1987 crash. Nomura first sold bonds with warrants to these favored clients at below-market prices. The clients were then asked to sell the securities back to the London subsidiary of a leading Japanese shipping firm, which earned a commission for performing this service. The shipping company then sold the bonds to a New York subsidiary of a major Japanese bank, which in turn transferred the securities (again for a commission) to a Hong Kong subsidiary of another leading Japanese bank. The Hong Kong subsidiary then sold the bonds with warrants back to the original client, which in turn sold them to Nomura in Tokyo. Following this most circuitous route, Nomura ultimately bought back from Showa Shell Sekiyu at a higher price the same bonds they had sold to the refiner one month earlier. This elaborate procedure, designed to mislead the tax man, shows why it is possible that some companies did not know they had been compensated. At any rate, this is what they claimed when the securities companies, after much professed reluctance about breaching client confidence, were forced at the end of July to name those they had compensated. In fact the brokers were happy to name the favored clients since it helped deflect attention away from them; they just could not admit it. A total of 228 companies were named as having been compensated by the Big Four. Two days later another 380 companies were named who had been compensated by thirteen second-tier securities firms. Well-known companies such as Matsushita, the giant consumer electronics firm, appeared on both lists. But most press attention focused on the embarrassing revelation that the government-run Pension Welfare Public Corporation topped the list of those compensated, having received ¥5.3 billion. Other public-sector entities, such as the police's and the public school teachers' mutual aid organizations, also featured in the lists.

Loss compensation may be bad business practice because it is ultimately self-defeating, but it is hardly unique to Japan. Nor is it so terrible. It could, for example, be argued that the brokers were only in essence giving their more important clients commission rebates. For if stockbroking commissions were deregulated in Japan, big corporate investors would end up paying lower commissions while small retail investors would pay more, as has been the experience in both New York and London. Likewise, the pervasive grip of soft commissions on Wall Street and increasingly in the City of London also suggests that Japan is not the only major country whose stock market is riddled with questionable practices that regulators openly tolerate, such as allowing stockbrokers to pay for services, such as a Reuters screen or telephone and tax bills, required by investment managers in return for receiving an agreed amount of commission. Soft commissions now account for over 30 percent of total stockbroking commissions on the New York Stock Exchange.

It also takes two to tango. It was hard to disbelieve Big Tabuchi when he finally testified before the Diet in September that the clients knew they were being compensated even if they did not quite appreciate all the technical details of how this compensation was being paid. Tabuchi also took this opportunity to make a further confession. He told the Diet that Nomura made compensation payments totaling ¥16 billion after the finance ministry's December 1989 decree specifically banned that practice. He said this was considered "unavoidable" in order to prevent trouble with clients that had suffered losses, and that Nomura had given top priority to closing the *eigyo tokkin* accounts. The former chairman added that these payments had been reported to the securities bureau of the finance ministry at the end of March 1990. Tabuchi's statement had the ring of truth.

Loss compensation may be rationalized as a legitimate business practice, however unwise. But it has now been made a criminal offense by a finance ministry and political establishment anxious to be seen to be doing the right thing. There are three key changes incorporated in the revision of the Japanese Securities Exchange Law. The first is a ban on discretionary trading accounts, like the *eigyo tokkin*, between securities companies and their customers. The second is a ban on guarantees against losses or even so-called yield guarantees, where a certain rate of return is promised. The third is a ban on clients' demanding compensation, guaranteed rates of return, or similar preferential treatment. The combined effect of these measures will be to eliminate a formerly widespread practice and so remove another of the institutional supports that helped maintain Japanese stock prices at inflated levels.

Loss compensation is a largely technical matter even if it does involve a flagrant breach of fairness by allowing some investors to be treated better than others. But there was nothing technical about the securities firms' open dealings with organized crime and the alleged manipulation of shares on the behalf of these criminal syndicates. That these deals had happened was itself not so surprising. But what was shocking was that Nomura and Nikko were caught *openly* dealing with gangsters. Traditionally in Japan there have been middlemen who served as a convenient and necessary buffer between legitimate business and the world of the *yakuza*. But a marked feature of the Bubble Economy was how these distinctions were blurred as the gangsters became more and more directly involved in the property and stock markets. They were attracted to these markets for the same reasons as others—the lure of fast money. Susumu Ishii, the former head of the Tokyo-based Inagawa-kai, Japan's second-largest crime syndicate, and the figure at the center of the scandals involving Nomura and Nikko, was the archetypal gangster who understood how to manipulate money and had learned to play the game of finance. After inheriting the leadership of the syndicate in 1986 from the gang's founder, Kakuji Inagawa, Ishii's strategy was to modernize the *yakuza* and diversify its sources of income away from traditional areas like extortion and prostitution into more legitimate fronts such as property, golf course development, and the stock market. Ishii even expanded into America, sometimes to the embarrassment of well-connected people. West Trusho, a company he controlled, paid a $250,000 finder's fee to Prescott Bush and Company for helping it buy for $5 million a 38 percent stake in Asset Management International Financing and Settlement, a financial-services firm. Prescott Bush is the brother of American president George Bush.

Nomura's and Nikko's crime was to help Ishii, who died conveniently of a cerebral hemorrhage in September 1991 before the sixty-seven-year-old gangster could be properly interrogated, to mount an apparent attempt to corner the shares of Tokyu Corporation, a major railroad company at the center of a group of companies whose combined annual revenues exceed ¥430 billion. Ishii purchased 29 million shares or 2 percent of Tokyu during six months in 1989. There are two controversial aspects to Nomura's and Nikko's roles in this case. The first is how they financed him; the second is whether they actively supported his attempt to corner the shares.

The brokers' role in financing him was blatant. Ishii borrowed a total of ¥36 billion from finance affiliates of Nomura and Nikko, pledging the Tokyu shares themselves as collateral. He raised an additional ¥38 billion from the securities firms directly and from ten other companies by selling them bogus membership rights to Iwama Country Club, a golf club Ishii was building in Ibaraki prefecture. They were bogus because the club is a public course with no private membership.

The question of stock manipulation is harder to prove, even though most people in the market knew something was up. This is not surprising, since Tokyu's stock rose 164 percent within a two-month period after Ishii began buying. There is also powerful evidence that Tokyu shares were heavily promoted throughout the Nomura branch system. In October 1989, for example, dealings in Tokyu shares accounted for 90 percent of turnover at several Nomura branches. Such damning evidence helps explain why Nobuhiko Matsuno, head of the finance ministry's securities bureau, told the Diet on August 31 that his ministry now suspected Nomura of having manipulated the shares of Tokyu for Ishii's benefit. Matsuno's revelation was deadly serious for Nomura, since share manipulation is a criminal offense in Japan. It also directly contradicted a July Tokyo Stock Exchange statement that its own investigations of dealings in Tokyu shares had turned up no evidence of hanky-panky, a conclusion that convinced no one. That Matsuno went public with the ministry's suspicions suggested that the finance ministry had concluded that criminal prosecutions resulting from continuing though separate police investigations of dealings in Tokyu were quite probable. These investigations were outside the finance ministry's control. The public prosecutor's office is more of an independent force than it is often given credit for in Japan. The finance ministry certainly does not have the authority to halt a prosecution just because it might find it politically expedient to do so. The real issue is whether the prosecutors can come up with enough hard evidence to justify prosecution. This remains in doubt since share manipulation is always hard to prove. Still, Matsuno's statement before the Diet can be interpreted as an acknowledgment by the securities bureau, the traditional defender of the securities industry, that the time had passed for cover-up and damage control. Instead, the bureau needed to join those calling for tougher action to hedge against the real possibility that some form of prosecution would be mounted.

Tokyu was not the only stock-manipulation case under police investigation. Following his dealings in Tokyu shares, Ishii also bought heavily (this time through Nikko) the shares of another company, Honshu Paper, before severe illness forced him to wind down his share-dealing activities. Thus Nikko also had to sweat about the prospect of facing a criminal-manipulation charge. The word from the prosecutors was that the evidence was clearer cut in the Honshu Paper case than in the Tokyu case.

In his own testimony to the Diet Big Tabuchi shed a little light on how Nomura had become involved with Ishii. He said that the contact who arranged the initial introduction with a Nomura director was a *sokaiya*. The *sokaiya* are a peculiarly Japanese phenomenon. They are professional extortionists who have traditionally made their living by threatening to disrupt companies' annual general meetings. They also for a handsome fee will make sure no one embarrasses senior management by asking awkward questions at these meetings. The powerful concept of face in Japan, the concern at all times to avoid confrontation or even mere embarrassment, makes the Japanese vulnerable to extortion and also peculiarly willing to pay for the services of extortionists. In recent years the *sokaiya* business has dwindled as a result of a revision of the commercial code that made it illegal for companies to pay for this particular sort of service. As ever, organized crime was quick to adapt to new circumstances. The property boom provided one wonderful opportunity. Gangsters have always been involved in property through the process of *jiage*. This is the forcible eviction by violence, or threats of violence, of tenants from a property. Japan's strict rent-control laws provide a natural demand for such services. With property prices booming it did not take the *yakuza* long to make the transition from *jiage* to speculating directly in property. The usual way is for *yakuza* interests to establish a presence in a building, say by renting a floor of office space through a front company. The word soon goes around about the new neighbors. Tenants vacate, and the price of the property falls. The *yakuza* can then buy in at distress-sale prices. Anyone who doubts the ability of the *yakuza* to make the average law-abiding Japanese scarper quickly should watch the reaction of bathers in a public *onsen*, or hot bath, when an unruly and intoxicated band of gangsters arrives on the scene. The author has had the dubious privilege of observing this phenomenon. The collection of *yakuza* who arrived at the *onsen* represented the lower end of the gangster order. Their bodies were covered with lurid tattoos, half their little fingers were missing, and they exuded a general air of disease combined with criminality. Almost immediately upon their arrival the law-abiding Japanese all fled the public bathing area, leaving the few assembled *gaijin* to sit, goggle, and trade weak jokes. This sort of popular reaction explains why banks have found it useful on occasions to employ the services of the *yakuza* by selling their bad debts to them at a discount. The gangster will then seek to collect the full face value of the loan, probably with a lot more success than the bank would have. Sometimes in return for such services the banks would make loans to finance or property companies set up as *yakuza* fronts. During the Bubble Economy, this money tended to go straight into the property and stock markets.

When the money went into the stock market securities companies naturally became involved. Taking gangsters' money and investing it could be a dangerous occupation for financial intermediaries. The celebrated case that provided a hint of the scandals to come concerned a former head of research at Cosmo Securities, who was found dead in a cement mixer in 1988 after disappearing with a colleague earlier that year. His mistake was to have agreed to manage money for the Osaka-based Yamaguchi-gumi, Japan's largest crime syndicate. Clearly his investment performance during the October 1987 crash had not pleased his clients. The *yakuza*, like many other unsophisticated investors in Japan, sometimes find it hard to take a loss. The Tokyo and Osaka offices of Morgan Stanley and Salomon Brothers have received telephone threats because of their futures-trading activities on several occasions since the stock market began falling. The assumption always made is that the callers represent *yakuza* interests who blame the stock market's woes and their own losses on the devious Americans.

[132]

The pervasive presence of organized crime within orderly Japan may seem anomalous, but in reality it is not. The *yakuza*, like everything else in Japan, has its allotted place within society and its own rights and obligations. Society tolerates this criminal underworld because it performs a necessary role. For example, Japan has almost no street crime to speak of, unlike most urban societies. One important reason for this astonishing fact is that the presence of the *yakuza* prevents free-lance criminals from plying their trade. But this is not their only function. Because Japan has so few lawyers, the services of the *yakuza* are often called upon to resolve disputes. This role is accentuated by a characteristic of Japanese society well described by Robert Delfs in the November 21, 1991, *Far Eastern Economic Review:* "The influence of the *yakuza*, particularly at times of national crisis, reflects an underlying trait in Japanese society—the tendency to resort to personal and extra-legal ways of solving problems when institutional methods fail." In 1989 Japan's National Police Agency (NPA) recorded more than 20,000 reported incidents of *yakuza* intervention in civil disputes. The gangsters were paid well for these services. The NPA estimates that Japan's criminal gangs, with approximately 87,000 members, generated a combined income of ¥1.3 trillion in 1989. This is probably an understatement.

But if the *yakuza* have their appointed and containable role, which until now has been almost legitimate and certainly tolerated within the confines of traditional Japan, they went well beyond that during the Bubble Economy, both in terms of their open dealings with legitimate business and their increasingly overt role as principals making investments, instead of intermediaries employed to expedite particular problems. This is why a new law was passed in May 1992 that designates the Yamaguchi-gumi and six other syndicates as criminal entities and makes illegal such acts as extortion and forcing people out of their properties. This legislation is the direct result of the scandals. It will have the potentially dangerous effect of forcing the *yakuza* underground.

The indiscretions of Nomura and Nikko pale into insignificance compared with the Itoman scandal. This took place in

Osaka, a city where there had always been far more crossover between the criminal underworld and organized business than in snooty Tokyo. The chairman of Sumitomo, one of Japan's most prominent banks, effectively allowed a gangster to be appointed to the board of Itoman, a prominent trading company. The gangster then proceeded to try to dismember that trading company in a manner that shocked Japan and severely damaged the reputation and financial clout of what had been regarded as the country's highest-flying bank in the 1980s.

Itoman had a respectable pedigree. The company was founded in Osaka in 1883 and became known for its expertise in trading textiles. Itoman had long been in the orbit of Sumitomo Bank, also of Osaka origin, even though the bank only owned a bit more than 3 percent of its shares. Itoman's troubles began during the 1973–74 recession; Sumitomo had to rescue Itoman when its mainstream textile business slumped. The bank official in charge of the bailout was Ichiro Isoda, then a vice-president but later the autocratic chairman of Sumitomo. Isoda sent one of his closest sidekicks and a protégé of his within the bank, Yoshihiko Kawamura, to become Itoman's new president. Kawamura revived the trading company's fortunes with the help of Sumitomo credit lines by diversifying into food and machinery. By 1988 sufficient financial stability had returned for Sumitomo to ask Itoman to return the favor and do some rescuing of its own. The needy target was Sugiya Shoji, a financially strapped Tokyo-based developer of one-room apartments whose main bank was Sumitomo. At the time, Sugiya Shoji had accumulated debts of some ¥250 billion. Sugiya Shoji was absorbed within the Itoman group and reemerged as the trading company's property affiliate. This marked the beginning of Itoman's aggressive and near-fatal foray into the world of property.

The really murky business commenced with the hiring in February 1990 of Suemitsu Ito. He was made head of Itoman's fast-growing property department and two months later was appointed a main board director. Ito had a background as a leading *jiageya*. He had helped the Itoman group purchase a prime Ginza site in 1987. The next year, Itoman had paid some $570 million for a plot of land in Aoyama, another prime central district of Tokyo. This deal fouled up in a bureaucratic impasse because it transpired that the finance ministry happened to own one-third of this particular parcel. One view is that this experience convinced Itoman of the need to employ the services of someone who could either anticipate such problems or at least speedily resolve them. But what was odd about the Itoman case was that, rather than just hire Ito's services by the hour or by the project as most Japanese property companies would have done, Itoman chose openly to promote this gangsterish figure to the important position of main board director.

The answer to this riddle was that Ito was really a front man for Ho Yong Chung, an ambitious self-made Osaka-based Korean businessman with underworld connections whom Kawamura had decided to trust and who proceeded to loot Itoman, ruthlessly borrowing an estimated ¥450 billion from Itoman and its various nonbank and insurance affiliates. Ho had become an increasingly well-known figure in the Kansai region that surrounds Osaka, having built up extensive interests in the local media as well as in property. A large macho figure with, according to one Japanese journalist who interviewed him, a fist like a baseball glove, Ho was no intellectual. But he had the native intelligence and cunning found in all successful con men. And like many would-be media barons before him, he was intent on using his business interests as a source of patronage to promote his political influence. Thus, in June 1989, Ho appointed two well-connected characters to the chairmanship and presidency of Kyoto Broadcasting (KBS), a regional television station that he controlled. Kunio Fukumoto was made chairman. He had been a cabinet secretary in the 1950s and in more recent years was best known as a major fund-raiser for Noboru Takeshita, the former Japanese prime minister who is still a hugely influential LDP politician. Takenobu Naito was made president of KBS Kyoto. Naito was a former political journalist who happened to be married to Takeshita's second daughter. Ho knew what he was doing. Takeshita is one of the two most powerful men in Japanese politics. The other is Shin Kanemaru, formally the

LDP's vice-chairman but in reality the ruling party's veteran godfather and ultimate behind-the-scenes political fixer. True to feudal tradition, Takeshita's first daughter is married to Kanemaru's first son.

Thus emboldened, Ho embarked on a looting rampage of Itoman. Ito's appointment to the trading company's board precipitated a wave of impetuous investments, many of which were highly dubious inside deals. In one case Itoman reportedly bought a plot of land in Hawaii from Ito's brother-in-law for $17 million more than it was really worth. In another deal Itoman extended loans to two paper companies owned by Ito's older brother. These companies then passed the loans on to an Osaka-based property developer. Ito also started buying art, which, like golf courses, was another favorite toy of the high rollers of the Bubble Economy. Ito bought more than two hundred paintings in Itoman's name. Some were bought from companies owned by Ho, who had acquired interests in property, newspapers, and television through aggressive borrowing. The paintings bought from *Kansai Shinbun,* a newspaper and one of Ho's companies, were later found to be worth only about half of what they had been officially valued at by an assessor from Seibu, a prominent Japanese department store. On investigation, Seibu found the valuation papers had been forged by an employee who had since left the company. Some other paintings were bought from Pisa, a Tokyo-based art company and a Saison affiliate where Isoda's oldest daughter, Sonoku Kukawa, worked. (The Saison group owns Seibu and other assets.) This is noteworthy because Kawamura has claimed under questioning that the main reason he hired Ito was because of the close relationship between Ito, Isoda, and his daughter. Kawamura has also said that he and Ito met with Isoda several times between June and August 1990 and on each occasion the Sumitomo chairman asked them to help his daughter. Meanwhile, the paintings were turned into promissory notes to creditors, converting them into a form of collateral against which to borrow cash and so circumvent finance ministry controls on property lending that had been introduced in April 1990.

Kawamura's and Itoman's ultimate undoing lay in a complete refusal to stop speculating long after most players saw the writing on the wall and had desperately begun to retrench. The company was already overcommitted to property at the end of 1989 before Kawamura decided to bet everything on Ho and had his front man, Ito, installed on the Itoman board. Ho also bought a 19 percent stake in Itoman. Even after Sumitomo finally became alarmed at what was going on inside the company, Itoman went on borrowing from smaller banks who assumed it was safe to lend because Sumitomo was known to be the trading company's main bank. In the six-month period between March and September 1990, Itoman's loans soared by ¥630 billion, an increase of 85 percent. Most of the borrowing was accounted for by Ho's and Ito's speculations, be they in art, golf courses, or land.

The end of Itoman's increasing lunacy was signaled by the launch in September 1990 of what would prove to be a five-month-long investigation of Sumitomo's accounts by the finance ministry. It was one of the longest official inspections in Japanese banking history. This official scrutiny soon prompted Isoda's resignation. He resigned in October, officially to take responsibility after a Sumitomo branch manager had been found to have extended an illegal loan to Mitsuhiro Kotani, the head of the well-known Ko-shin speculative investment group who was under indictment for violating securities laws in a different case. The authorities were well aware of the mess at Itoman when they signaled that Isoda must go. His humiliating departure marked the end of what had been a long autocratic rule over the bank. Isoda had become known as the Emperor within Sumitomo during his thirteen years in the top post. He personified the aggressive, go-getting, risk-taking Sumitomo culture that was lauded uncritically by all manner of pundits during the credit-mad 1980s. Sumitomo had once been the bank most others tried to emulate, but this is no longer so. Sumitomo will spend several years working its way out of the Itoman problem. Because of Sumitomo's role as main bank, the Itoman affair has left it shouldering bad debts of at least ¥500 billion and probably much more as it is obliged to rescue Itoman, with estimated total debts of ¥1.4 trillion, for the second time in twenty years, though this occasion is on a far grander scale than the first. Unsworn testimony by Sumitomo president Sotoo Tatsumi to the Diet in September 1991 reveals how costly it can be to be a main bank in the event of a corporate debacle like Itoman's. Tatsumi said the bank's loans to Itoman grew from ¥165 billion in September 1990 to ¥553 billion in July 1991 as Sumitomo was obliged to take over other banks' bad debts.

The Itoman affair will be played out for years in the courts. Kawamura was arrested in July 1991 and charged with improperly buying Itoman shares between October 1989 and November 1990 with loans obtained from Itoman subsidiaries in a Robert Maxwell–style attempt to support the stock price and fend off Sumitomo pressure to force him out. Because he refused to step down voluntarily Kawamura eventually had to be sacked formally in January 1991 at a specially summoned emergency board meeting. This was a rare occurrence in Japan. Meanwhile, Ito had resigned in November following widespread press reports of Itoman's woes. There were several other arrests alongside Kawamura's. Sadamu Takagaki, a former Itoman vice-president, was charged as an accomplice in Kawamura's share-buying schemes. Ho Yong Chung (the key figure), Ito, and two of Ho's associates were arrested simultaneously in August 1991 and charged with breach of trust in connection with art deals totaling ¥56 billion and with using 145 valuation certificates forged in the name of Seibu Department Stores. Public prosecutors claim that Itoman had suffered a loss of some ¥33 billion from buying artwork at inflated prices. Subsequently, prosecutors filed new charges against Ho, Ito, and their accomplices, charging them with conspiring to use money borrowed by Itoman for their own personal purposes. In one case Ito is alleged to have spent ¥23 billion of loans raised by Itoman to pay off personal debts he had incurred buying land in Tokyo's Ginza district. By then Fukumoto and Naito had long resigned from Kyoto Broadcasting, doubtless embarrassed by their proximity to this scandal, as Takeshita must also have been. The Itoman arrests followed months of work by prosecutors, during the course of which they interviewed more than a thousand people and searched some 140 different locations. Meanwhile, perhaps the biggest victim of the whole affair was Yoshikuni Nato, head of Itoman's Nagoya branch, who was found dead in his bath on December 1, 1991, having apparently decided to kill himself before the finance ministry's investigators closed in. Nato left a note blaming trouble at work. He had joined Itoman from Sumitomo in Kawamura's wake.

# 7

# Banking Scandals

The details of the scandals that engulfed the securities industry may have been old hat to insiders. That was not the case with the revelations that tarnished the reputations of several of Japan's leading banks.

The discovery of forged certificates of deposit and the billions of dollars of phony credit that resulted came as a profound shock to most observers, including senior officials at the Bank of Japan and the Ministry of Finance, who had been operating under the delusion that they knew what was going on in the key industry over which they presided. Yet there had been hints earlier for those prepared to look that there was something terribly rotten with Japan's credit system. Take, for example, a little-noticed scam whose exposure merited only a few newspaper inches in September 1990. It concerned the case of Keiko Fujinori, a fifty-seven-year-old spinster who was alleged to have stolen ¥1.9 billion between 1973 and 1989 from the small Tokyo credit union where she was employed. This financial institution had a total of only ¥10 billion in deposits and only three branches. According to Tokyo police, Fujinori's favored ruses included falsely canceling depositors' accounts and making up fictitious loans. Doubtless her acts would have continued to go unnoticed had not the Mukojima Credit Association, for which she was a deputy branch manager, merged with a bigger bank. It is remarkable that a single employee could have absconded with the equivalent of nearly 20 percent of a financial institution's total deposits.

This incident served as but a prologue. The banking scandals did not formally commence until July 25, 1991, when Taizo Hashida, chairman and president of Fuji Bank, admitted in a public statement that three of the bank's Tokyo branches were implicated in the issuing of forged certificates of deposit with a face value of ¥260 billion. These phony CDs had been used during the previous four years as collateral by twenty-three unnamed property companies to enable them to borrow ¥260 billion from fourteen nonbanks. As usual, these property companies were suspected by police investigators of having *yakuza* connections.

Fuji, Japan's fourth-largest bank and a pillar of the Tokyo business establishment, said it only became aware of the scam when some of the borrowers defaulted on interest payments and the nonbank lenders inquired about their collateral. Fuji's response was to take over all the nonbanks' debt and sack four of its own employees who were implicated in the forgeries. Hashida claimed that the bank had suffered an effective loss of only ¥27 billion, which represented the portion of the loans that was unsecured. The rest, it is presumably hoped, is secured on something stronger than forged CDs. But evidence of more hanky-panky at Fuji emerged the same week when it was revealed that 400,000 shares of Fusuke, a sock-making company whose shares had been regularly cornered by speculators, had disappeared from Fuji's Hibiya branch in central Tokyo, prompting concern that this was part of the collateral Fuji hoped to secure the rest of the loans with. Meanwhile, Fuji filed police complaints against three of the sacked employees: Minoru Nakamura, a manager at the Akasaka branch in central Tokyo, Hideo Sato, an assistant manager at the same branch, and Kazuaki Kanno, senior manager at the Hibiya branch. Nakamura and Sato were duly arrested in September, accused of fraud and forgery, six weeks after Fuji had filed the criminal complaints. Also arrested was Akira Akagi, president of Marusho Kosan, a Tokyo property company that was directly implicated in the scheme since some of the loans raised were funneled to the company. Unlike the securities scandals, no one pretended that the activities were anything but illegal. There was embarrassment all around, for this was not the sort of activity to expose to an outside world always ready to seize on Japan's weak spots.

At the time of its disclosure the Fuji affair looked like an aberration, an egregious example of criminal wrongdoing. But this impression only lasted a couple of days. Forging certificates of deposit was, it seemed, almost a common practice. Within days of Fuji's announcement two other city banks, Tokai Bank and Kyowa Saitama Bank, admitted to having unearthed similar transgressions. Tokai disclosed that Toru Morimoto, deputy manager of its Akihabara branch in Tokyo, had admitted to issuing fake CDs to several companies for use as collateral to borrow ¥63 billion from various nonbanks, including Orix, Japan's biggest leasing company. Likewise, Kyowa Saitama announced that Kazuo Toyama, yet another branch manager, had forged ¥8 billion worth of phony CDs for the benefit of two Tokyo-based companies, a property firm and a golf course development company. Both frauds were again only discovered when the borrowers failed to make interest payments and the nonbank lenders contacted the banks regarding the worth of their collateral.

These three banking scams coming one after the other made it hard to believe the banks' claims that they knew nothing about the forgeries until the nonbanks made their inquiries. If true, it suggests at best incredibly sloppy management. Even for a bank as big as Fuji, ¥260 billion, a sum equivalent to some $2 billion, is a lot of phony credit to let go unmonitored. The forgeries looked suspiciously like a devious scheme to get around government controls on lending to property companies, using nonbanks as the chosen conduit. If a would-be borrower could persuade a reputable bank to provide evidence of a deposit he was free to borrow from other banks or nonbanks using that deposit as collateral. Hence the value of forged CDs. Subsequent inquiries established that Nakamura's boss at Fuji's Akasaka branch had known about the forged CDs as early as February 1989 but chose not to report the transgression to the head office. Even if senior management did not specifically endorse such illegal acts, by turning a blind eye they contributed to an atmosphere where employees were encouraged to take shortcuts in the rush to lend money. Branch managers were given asset targets that they were determined to meet at all costs. They were also given a lot of freedom by the head office as to how to achieve those targets.

This certainly seems to have been the case at Fuji, which has been mired in more than its fair share of scandals and which seems to have been led astray by a desperate and disastrous attempt to imitate the success of Sumitomo Bank. For example, Fuji was also caught up in the Itoman scandal. Fuji introduced thirty-eight of its clients to Osaka Fumin Shinyo Kumiai, a small Osaka credit union. These clients proceeded to deposit ¥134.5 billion in this institution. Without their knowledge, their money was duly lent on to the infamous Ito of Itoman and through him to his puppet master, Ho Yong Chung. Hashida later claimed in unsworn testimony to the Diet that Fuji's clients deposited their funds in the Osaka credit union because they were seeking a higher interest rate and that Fuji did not know that the deposits had been lent on to the former Itoman director. Yet Fuji's general conduct in this instance hardly seemed to pass the proverbial smell test, and the authorities made Fuji contribute ¥100 billion to the bailout of Osaka Fumin organized by the Osaka prefectural government. The credit union had been badly pillaged. Its bad loans totaled some ¥90 billion, almost half its assets.

Fuji's obsession with Sumitomo stemmed from the inroads the Osaka-based bank had made in Fuji's Tokyo home market. In its zeal to match Sumitomo's success Fuji tried to ape its competitor's aggression. Fuji's problem was that its traditionalist, almost gentlemanly culture meant it could only foul up when it sought to copy Sumitomo's aggressive approach to business. Fuji did not know how to be Sumitomo. Yet in trying to be something it was not, always as bad a mistake in business as it is in life, the bank lost sight of its own culture. This contrasts with Mitsubishi Bank, which never forsook its traditionally strong credit culture during the 1980s. This may be partly because its chairman and former president, Kazuo Ibuki, rose up through the division of the bank that assesses credit risk. To make a bad loan earns employees a black mark within the bank and can harm a person's career. Consequently, Mitsubishi probably has the lowest exposure to bad debt of all the major city banks within Japan. It is the bank others will seek to emulate during the 1990s, just as they sought to emulate Sumitomo in the 1980s.

Sumitomo is Nomura's equivalent in the banking world: a hard-driven army with fiercely commercial instincts. By contrast, Fuji is a bank full of members of the upper class. Some 55 percent of its executive officers and 80 percent of its representative directors are graduates of the elite Tokyo University, according to *Diamond* magazine, a form of alumni penetration only exceeded by the even more establishment Industrial Bank of Japan. It is interesting that the Fuji branch managers who were dismissed and arrested for forging the CDs were not graduates of Tokyo University. The word within Fuji is that since the men were not members of the Tokyo University old boys' club, they felt under more pressure to make a mark and prove themselves in this most hierarchical of institutions.

A hint of what it is like to work inside a bank like Fuji was provided by a book published at the same time the scandals were making front-page news. It was written by Akio Koiso, a labor activist and career banker who had worked at Fuji for thirty-eight years and who was still in charge of handling the cash coming into the bank's Asakusa branch in eastern Tokyo. Koiso is a refreshing oddity in Japan, an individual who is prepared to stick his neck out. Titled *The Report of a Fuji Bank Employee,* his book contrasts the grand expansionist international aspirations of Japan's city banks during the 1980s with the feudal way they ran their own organizations. It also details Fuji's obsession with Sumitomo. (At Fuji's 1980 centenary celebrations, employees were urged to keep working until they "urinated blood.") According to Koiso, the regular working day at Fuji is from 8:00 A.M. to 9:00 P.M., yet overtime pay is limited to twenty hours a month. Employees' performance is assessed by strict numerical scoring. Koiso's outspokenness was too embarrassing for Fuji to ignore. Before publication of the book Koiso was summoned to the head office and told by the chief of the bank's personnel department that he would be disciplined, and that the severity of the punishment, which might include dismissal, would depend on the book's contents. Koiso says he told the manager to fire him "if you can." Koiso's evident self-confidence stemmed from his knowledge that Fuji dared not sack a man whom it must have regarded as a major troublemaker because of public support and the increasingly sleazy reputation of Japanese banks. After all, the book was published at a time when Hashida was poised to resign to take responsibility for the forged CD scandal (though like his Nomura counterparts he would stay on as an adviser). It was also hard to disbelieve Koiso when he said that he had received lots of private verbal support within the bank for his literary efforts.

For a few brief weeks the Fuji scandal enjoyed the dubious merit of being Japan's largest-ever bank fraud. But it was soon outdone by perhaps the most extraordinary of all the weird goings-on exposed by the bursting of the Bubble Economy. This was the larger-than-life tale of Industrial Bank of Japan's involvement with the mysterious Nui Onoue, the sixty-one-year-old spinster owner of two Osaka restaurants. IBJ and its affiliates lent at the peak of their exposure the colossal sum of ¥240 billion to Onoue, who became in the late 1980s the biggest individual speculator in the Tokyo stock market. The details of Onoue's portfolio at the prime of her investment career are remarkable. She owned 3.1 million shares in IBJ itself, making her the bank's largest individual shareholder. She also owned a collection of other blue chips, including 8 million shares in Dai-Ichi Kangyo Bank, 2 million shares in Sumitomo Bank, 6 million shares in Tokyo Electric Power, 3 million in Fuji Heavy Industries, and 3 million in Toshiba, to list just part of her portfolio. Her buy orders were on the scale of major institutional investors. For example, on the single day of April 24, 1991, Onoue purchased through Universal Securities, a Daiwa Securities affiliate, ¥120 billion worth of shares, according to the May 1991 edition of *Tokyo Insider* (since renamed *Tokyo Insideline*), a monthly publication that first disclosed the story of IBJ's megafinancing of Onoue more than three months before it became the talk of Japan.

Even before there was any hint of criminal activity, the sheer size of IBJ group lending to Onoue seemed unbelievable. Onoue was hardly an established figure, and the source of her wealth was shrouded in mystery. Onoue's early adulthood appears to have been spent as a waitress in bars and restaurants in the bustling Minami entertainment area of Osaka. With the help of financial support provided by an unnamed business executive, Onoue bought two neighboring restaurants in Osaka, called the Egawa and the Daikokuya. By the late 1980s Onoue had built up a reputation as a heavy-hitting investor and her restaurants were frequented by stockbrokers anxious to procure her business. Her technique was not to trade in and out of the market but rather to buy huge holdings of blue-chip shares, especially bank shares. To further her image as a stock market guru Onoue would hold midnight rites at one of the restaurants with the apparent aim of seeking financial advice from the divinities. Onoue claimed to be a follower of *mikkyō*, an esoteric Buddhist cult. This enhanced the aura of mystery that surrounded her. Stockbrokers who wanted her business made sure they attended these nocturnal sessions, but no one seemed to have any idea exactly how this woman, who was known as the Dark Lady of Osaka, came by all her money, though naturally in such curious circumstances rumors abounded.

Onoue was a much talked about figure in the securities world of Osaka thanks to the money she threw around and the brokering commissions she generated for those fortunate enough to receive her business. But that was as far as her reputation extended until her name became as well known as any in Japan in August 1991 when she was arrested for obtaining loans with false documents, including ¥340 billion worth of fake CDs issued in the name of the Toyo Shinkin Bank, a small Osaka credit union. Onoue was also found to be facing personal bankruptcy with estimated debts of more than ¥400 billion, the result of the stock market's crash.

The amount of money involved in the fraud boggles the imagination, as does the role played by IBJ, which to its intense embarrassment was Onoue's chief source of credit. According to its own version of events, IBJ says that its relationship with Onoue began in 1987 when she walked into its Osaka branch and began buying large amounts of IBJ debentures. The debentures were bought with bank checks, not cash. IBJ stresses this point because of as-yet unproven allegations about money laundering and Onoue's involvement with organized crime. Onoue proceeded to borrow heavily from IBJ using the debentures she owned as collateral. The bank liked this arrangement because it seemed both safe and profitable, since it was effectively being paid to lend Onoue her own money. This activity continued on a grand scale. At the peak of her relationship with the bank, Onoue had borrowed a total of ¥240 billion from IBJ and its affiliates. IBJ lent ¥90 billion directly; ¥80 billion was lent by IBJ Leasing and ¥70 billion by IBJ Finance. This money was lent against a peak of ¥290 billion worth of IBJ debentures owned by Onoue. IBJ felt that it was protected so long as the bank lent Onoue less than the amount of IBJ debentures she owned. At the time the bank had no limit on the number of its own debentures that could be sold to any one individual, a policy that has since been scrapped.

However, the scale of the lending still seems extraordinary given IBJ's professed ignorance about how Onoue acquired her wealth. But up to this point nothing underhanded seems to have occurred. The murky business only began in April 1991, at least according to IBJ's account. After that date Onoue was allowed by IBJ's Osaka branch on three separate occasions to swap temporarily her IBJ debentures with CDs issued in the name of Toyo Shinkin Bank (the CDs later turned out to be forged). The excuse she made on the first occasion was that she had to show the debentures to the tax inspectors. In fact Onoue used the IBJ debentures temporarily in her possession to borrow funds elsewhere, mainly from non-banks, which would have regarded IBJ debentures as the safest collateral. It was only on the fourth occasion in August when she was yet again allowed to exchange the collateral that the fraud surfaced. IBJ says it only found out the CDs were phony on August 9, when Onoue confessed all to the senior management at Toyo Shinkin, who at once informed IBJ.

Onoue was arrested, as was Tomomi Maekawa, Toyo Shinkin's fifty-eight-year-old Osaka branch manager, who was charged with issuing to Onoue ¥340 billion worth of fake CDs between October 1990 and April 1991. These were pledged as collateral to obtain that amount in loans from about a dozen financial institutions, mainly local Osaka nonbanks. Revelation of the scandal set off alarm bells at the Bank of Japan, where officials moved quickly to contain the damage stemming from what was, by a wide margin, Japan's biggest-ever banking fraud. The authorities took no chances. Cash was physically transported from Tokyo to Osaka to make sure Toyo Shinkin could meet all claims by alarmed depositors wanting their money back. The central bank and the depositors had every reason to be concerned since the size of the loans made against the credit union's forged CDs was almost as great as Toyo Shinkin's total deposits. It was also more than half the cash reserves held by Japan's deposit insurance fund.

IBJ's own direct exposure was not so great when the scandal broke. The bank explains this by saying that it began reducing its loans to Onoue from October 1990 on after rumors started circulating that she had "underground" connections. Consequently, IBJ and its affiliates were left with a total exposure of only ¥60 billion at the time of her arrest. Still, this probably understates the bank's final exposure. IBJ is likely to be held responsible for some of the other bad debts incurred, as a result of its releasing the collateral even if it was only on a temporary basis. Officials at the Bank of Japan take the view that IBJ's imprudence in letting go of the debentures puts it under a moral obligation to make good some of Onoue's bad debts. IBJ's argument is that Sanwa Bank should be held principally responsible since Sanwa is Toyo Shinkin's main bank (a claim Sanwa might dispute) and Maekawa was a former Sanwa employee. That may be, say central bankers. But, they contend, the pertinent point is that IBJ is Onoue's main bank. This judgment seems eminently sensible. Even if IBJ's own version of events is accepted, it is a total breach of prudential banking practice to release collateral on no less than four occasions to any single borrower, especially one with a shrouded past and possible mob connections. Collateral is meant to be locked up in a bank vault and not released until the loan is repaid. Otherwise it can be borrowed against many times over. To maintain that this fundamental lapse in good banking practice only occurred as a result of slack management, as IBJ does, is to ask people to believe too much. This is also why it is hard to accept that IBJ was "fooled," the official explanation given by Yoh Kurosawa, the bank's smooth-talking president, to the Diet in September. Still, even this official version of events caused great damage to IBJ's illustrious reputation within Japan. "Kogin," as the bank is known in Japan, was supposed to be the smartest of the smart.

It is also a little hard to accept at face value IBJ's statements that there was no relationship whatsoever between Onoue and any of IBJ's directors or former directors. The bank does not deny that Onoue met president Kurosawa on four separate occasions. Two of these are described as courtesy calls to an important client. Another was when Kurosawa had dinner in one of Onoue's restaurants with his family while on holiday and, according to an IBJ spokesman, paid for the meal himself. The final occasion was on August 8, when Onoue visited Kurosawa at IBJ's head office in Tokyo's financial district when, according to IBJ, she came to reassure him personally that she had no *yakuza* ties. Remarkably, it was the very next day, back in Osaka, that Onoue detonated the bombshell by owning up to Toyo Shinkin about the forged CDs. Whether four separate meetings amount to more than a formal business relationship is a matter of interpretation. But one point is sure. A visit to the site of Onoue's now closed restaurants suggests that Kurosawa's own presence there, even if he was on vacation, should at the very least have given him pause for thought both about the size of IBJ's own exposure to this individual and about how Onoue acquired the wherewithal to buy all those IBJ debentures.

The restaurants are located in a rather seedy area of the city known by locals as the home of love hotels and *yakuza* offices. Behind the Egawa is a lurid seven-story love hotel called Emotion

House. Opposite is one of Osaka's few Christian churches. To one side is a strip club named Igirisu, or England, advertised by flashing light bulbs and a Union Jack flag. On the other side of the restaurants is an even more incongruous site, though on a similar theme. This is an old-fashioned British-style cloth tailor. Its presence is advertised by a shotgun, a red grenadier's jacket and busby hat, and an old-fashioned white dinner jacket in the shop window. The Japanese proprietor of this establishment learned his craft as an apprentice, spending five years in London's Saville Row, and speaks fluent cockney English.

This is the strange context in which Japan's biggest-ever banking fraud was set. Why did IBJ get so deeply involved with such a questionable figure? One possible clue to the tangled affair was suggested by *Tokyo Insider*. Onoue comes from an area close to Wakayama prefecture near Osaka. Officially she claims she was born in Kyoto prefecture and graduated from the elite Nara Women's University. The latter claim is certainly not true since that educational institution has no record of her attendance. Wakayama is known to have a large and closely knit community of *burakumin*, the descendants of the untouchables of Japan's feudal society. Wakayama is famous among Japanese eye specialists for a genetic disorder caused by extensive inbreeding, a feature common to this community. The family of Kisabura Ikeura, IBJ's former chairman, patron of Kurosawa, and before the scandal the single most powerful individual within the bank, also came from Wakayama, as did another IBJ director, Shuichiro Tamaki. Tamaki is said to be a friend of Mahito Kamei, the manager of IBJ's Osaka branch that actually lent the money to Onoue. The extent to which these leading lights had relationships, if any, with the *burakumin* community in Wakayama is impossible to prove. IBJ categorically denies any such ties. The bank's official line is that no one in IBJ knew Onoue until she walked into the Osaka branch and purchased the debentures. A bank spokesman does concede that she was famous in the Osaka area for being a rich woman, but when asked how she became so rich the reply was, "We really don't know. This was something mysterious to us also."

The possible Wakayama connection touches on one of the

most sensitive of subjects in Japan, the *burakumin*. There are said to be about 2 million *burakumin* living in Japan, many clustered in the Osaka area. They are ethnically indistinguishable from other Japanese but are the target of great prejudice. It is routine, for example, for parents to hire private detectives to find out whether a prospective son-in-law or daughter-in-law is contaminated. This discrimination means that the more aggressive entrepreneurial businessmen who rise out of the *burakumin* ranks often feel compelled to use questionable methods to acquire influence, since the doors of the establishment would otherwise be shut to them. Hiromasa Ezoe, the entrepreneur who built up his company Recruit Cosmos by pioneering job-placement publishing in Japan and whose company later lent its name to a major political scandal that forced the resignation of Noboru Takeshita as prime minister in the late 1980s, is widely believed to have come from this community. By their very nature such things are impossible to confirm formally in opaque Japan, but such links would certainly help explain why Ezoe felt the need to dole out so much money to politicians in an attempt to acquire influence. Many of the more aggressive upstart entrepreneurs or plain speculators who rose to prominence during the bubble years were also said to come from the *burakumin* community. Whether true or not, such rumors fester because of the continuing Japanese predilection for pretending in public that the *burakumin* do not exist. All talk of the *burakumin* is off-limits in Japan. Even to use the word in writing in Japanese is considered offensive and is to invite threats of blackmail or worse from this community. Japan, remember, is a society where extortion is widely practiced.

This is clear from the experience of *Tokyo Insider*'s Takao Toshikawa as a result of publishing the article on the alleged Wakayama connection. He was approached by Kunio Fukumoto, the behind-the-scenes political fixer and the man Ho of Itoman fame had appointed as chairman of Kyoto Broadcasting. Fukumoto's current formal occupation is president of the Fuji International Art Gallery in Tokyo's Marunouchi district, but he is better known in political circles as a fund-raiser for former prime minister Takeshita. He is still active in the dominant Takeshita faction of the LDP, working for Takeshita personally, which is why Ho was anxious to cultivate a relationship. It is the Takeshita faction that pulls the strings of whoever is nominally head of the LDP and therefore, given Japan's protracted period of one-party rule, prime minister of the country. Thus, Kaifu remained in power only as long as he suited the purposes of the Takeshita faction and, most important, Takeshita himself. This meant primarily doing what he was told and not stepping out of line, an odd state of affairs to say the least for a premier whose appointment had been endorsed at the polls. Fukumoto advised Toshikawa to take care what he wrote about IBJ. The explanation may be that Toshikawa had been investigating other potential scandals, as he had, the disclosure of which concerned IBJ's leading lights. Evidently, given Fukumoto's interest, that possible disclosure concerned Takeshita more than the saga of Onoue.

If the extent to which personal relationships played a part, if any, in explaining why IBJ lent so much money to Onoue is still unclear, the source of her original seed capital remains equally mysterious. Speculation abounds. On September 2, 1991, Yoshiaki Ariki, an employee of National Leasing Company, an affiliate of Matsushita, the giant electronics concern, was indicted. Ariki's alleged offense was to have replaced securities lodged as collateral by Onoue with forged CDs. This arrest served to fuel the already widespread speculation that Onoue's original patron was Masaharu Matsushita, chairman of the giant consumer electronics firm and son-in-law of the firm's founder. Again there is no evidence to support this theory. Japanese journalists say that since Onoue has been in custody she has told prosecutors during interrogation that her original patron was not Matsushita but a member of the Ishibashi family, which runs Daiwa House, a major home building company. This is impossible to confirm, since the executive in question is now dead. But one point is clear: the record shows that Onoue is a great liar.

The Onoue affair ended for IBJ the same way it did for other financial institutions caught up in scandals. On October 22, 1991, more than two months after the scandal broke, the once unthinkable happened. The chairman of IBJ, Kaneo Nakamura, and another senior official resigned in disgrace. There was a reason for the delay in the resignations. IBJ had been hoping to postpone the by now familiar bowing of heads and ritual apologies until the Osaka public prosecutor's office had concluded its investigation of the Onoue affair lest any new skeletons were discovered in the closet. It was also not easy in faction-riven IBJ to reach a consensus on who should make the sacrifice. But in the end it was decided that internal morale was deteriorating too fast to permit further procrastination. The bank's most venerable elder statesman, Sohei Nakayama, who is now IBJ's senior adviser and was himself a former chairman and president, is thought to have played the key role in deciding that both the current chairman, Nakamura, and the preceding chairman, Ikeura (formally described as director and "counselor") should go. Kamei, general manager of the Osaka branch also resigned, as did Shuji Yamamoto, the Osaka branch head before him. Kazuo Suzuki, a former deputy general manager of the Osaka branch, was suspended for two months for what an IBJ spokesman described at the time as "immoral, inappropriate behavior as a banker." Suzuki had been questioned by the prosecutors about borrowing ¥90 million personally from Onoue, or about twice the amount he could expect to receive on retirement. In his defense Suzuki had apparently argued that the money was no gift but had been properly lent against collateral, but he seems to have been in rather deep. The Friday before Onoue was arrested Suzuki had contacted the Bank of Tokyo's Osaka branch to request that the bank issue a debenture of ¥20 billion. Suzuki said he would introduce a customer who wished to be given the debenture on the bank's receipt of a check. The Bank of Tokyo's Osaka branch sensibly declined this strange request, saying it would be necessary to wait until the check had cleared before issuing such a debenture. At that point an obviously desperate Suzuki became angry and was told to go to another bank. When the news broke the next week, the Bank of Tokyo's Osaka branch telephoned the contact number Suzuki had given. It was the number of one of Onoue's restaurants.

The decision that both Ikeura and Nakamura should go made sense. Ikeura was chairman when the initial business contacts were made with Onoue, and Nakamura was president. Moreover, Ikeura and Nakamura headed the two rival factions within the bank. It was doubly appropriate that Ikeura should go since in many people's opinion he was IBJ's main problem. Although he was no longer chairman he had continued to wield more power than any other single individual in the bank (including Nakamura). Indeed, IBJ was sometimes described as a one-man dictatorship. This was dangerous since Ikeura was no longer formally responsible to the board for his actions, since he was not chairman. Ikeura's power base stemmed from his strength of character and his role as kingmaker. Most present IBJ directors owe their positions on the board to his patronage, including Kurosawa himself, who is generally considered an Ikeura yes-man. Ikeura became president of IBJ in 1975 and assumed the chairmanship in 1984. Nakamura, his successor in both positions, did not have the same kind of powerful support group within the bank, since he was not so political a figure. But he was supported by the growing number of younger modernists, especially those who had worked abroad and had learned a different way of doing things. They disliked Ikeura's old-fashioned godfather-like approach, which stemmed from his opinion that he personally had taken care of IBJ's position in Japan thanks to the value of his own contacts with the finance ministry and the LDP political leadership (Ikeura is a close friend of Takeshita's). Ikeura represented the feudal past, albeit a powerful past. His resignation therefore delivered a firm message throughout the bank that his time was over. Yet Ikeura probably agreed to step down only because he received something in return. He protected his protégé Kurosawa, who remains in the president's job for now despite the embarrassment of his four meetings with Onoue. Whether he stays in power, resigns, or gets kicked upstairs as a figurehead chairman will depend on IBJ avoiding fresh scandals or financial debacles. That cannot be guaranteed, because the bank seems to have been less wise than many of its competitors during the bubble years. Onoue was not the only customer to whom IBJ's

Osaka branch lent unwisely. IBJ is heavily exposed to the FOKAS companies in Osaka. It is the biggest lender, and so risks being deemed main banker, to Fuji Juken. It is also one of the main lenders to Asahi Juken. Both these companies' huge debts have had to be rescheduled. But perhaps most embarrassing, the IBJ group is also the biggest lender to Sueno Kosan, another troubled property company with group debts of ¥650 billion. In Osaka this company is generally linked with the Yamaguchi-gumi syndicate, through its president Kenichi Sueno. Police have investigated this alleged relationship though they have yet to come up with any proof. This is not for want of trying. Sueno was arrested in Fukuoka, a provincial city, in August 1991 and charged with a technical violation of a building code. He was subsequently detained for twenty days for questioning by the department of the Fukuoka police that deals with gangsters. Sueno Kosan owns several buildings that house nightclubs, cabarets, and similar establishments. Like Onoue, Sueno Kosan is not the sort of client with which IBJ is traditionally associated. The bank's exposure to property is also not limited to its direct loans. Its main property affiliate, Kowa Real Estate, has itself borrowed more money than any other Japanese property company, according to Tokyo Shoko Research. Kowa had debts of ¥1.16 trillion at the end of 1989. It owned ninety-five office buildings in Japan and thirty-five apartment buildings. It has also been aggressively investing abroad and at home in the Tokyo stock market.

It may seem unfair to single out IBJ since many Japanese banks have fouled up badly in recent years as a result of lax credit practices, as indeed have leading banks all over the world. And its two rival long-term credit banks, Long-Term Credit Bank and Nippon Credit Bank, may arguably be in even worse shape. But the significance of the IBJ scandals is that the bank's recent troubles contrast so markedly with the prestige traditionally accorded it as an institution and with its historic role as the main financial motor of Japanese heavy industry in the 1950s and early 1960s. The bank's core problem is that because of this traditional emphasis on heavy industry it missed out on financing the higher growth businesses of more recent vintage, primarily electronics. And unlike the city banks, IBJ doesn't have a large branch network and thus a secure retail deposit base. So when Japan went crazy on credit in the late 1980s exclusive IBJ found itself forced to chase fringe loan business within Japan. Bankers say it was even known for aggressively soliciting *sarakin*, Japan's legalized loan sharks, in a bid to lend them money. This aggression went hand in hand with equally aggressive property lending in America, as described earlier. Yet despite this accumulated credit risk and an anachronistic franchise, investors are still willing to pay an extraordinary premium for IBJ shares as if there remains some special magic to the name and the organization. This was a sure sign that some excesses still lingered, that the bubble has not yet burst completely.

# 8

# Bureaucrats and Politicians

To understand the authority of Japan's bureaucracy, and the Ministry of Finance in particular, it is necessary to comprehend the poverty of its politics. Government bureaucrats like to say they do not mind if Japanese politicians are venal, second-rate, and generally self-serving since that leaves them free to get on with running the country as they see fit.

Japanese politics is indeed as feudal as its financial system, if not more so. The real political rivalry is not between political parties offering competing policies but between LDP members competing for votes from the same constituency. Hence the development of factional politics, of which the Takeshita faction is the most powerful. The main purpose of each faction is to raise money for election campaigns. The stock market has historically been the favorite vehicle for doing this. This is the origin of the sleazy money politics associated with the Recruit shares-for-favors scandal.

At present there are 130 constituency boundaries that each elect three, four, or five candidates. Present constituency boundaries favor rural districts. The game is therefore for politicians to compete to see who can bag the best building project or, even better, the next *shinkansen* (bullet train) line, for the most remote rural area. This rural bias entrenches the feudal nature of Japanese politics, since politicians inherit constituencies rather as grandees in eighteenth-century England sat for rotten boroughs. One-third of the LDP members of the lower house of the Japanese Diet, the more powerful of the two legislative chambers, are either the sons of politicians or are married to the daughters of politicians.

It is in the context of this political circus, or rather in spite of it, that the bureaucracy wields its power. At the apex of that bureaucracy is the Ministry of Finance, which sees itself as the true guardian of the national interest. If there is such a thing as a center of power, and it is a moot question whether the concept has any real meaning in Japan, this institution is the nearest thing to it. The source of its power is understandable. The Ministry of Finance collects tax revenues and draws up the national budget. It also recruits the best talent, who like to refer to themselves self-consciously and somewhat absurdly as "the best and the brightest." The finance ministry takes about twenty-five graduates every year and it is not unusual for up to 95 percent to come from the elite Tokyo University, with a smattering from Kyoto University. When these young men (there are only one or two token women) first arrive their working conditions are frugal in the extreme. The Ministry of Finance has a laudable tradition of austerity, an admirable trait given its role as watchdog over the public purse. It also is in stark contrast to the conspicuous consumption so brazenly on display during the period of the Bubble Economy. The finance ministry was, for example, the last government ministry to put tiles on its fortress-like walls. First-time visitors to the ministry are astonished to encounter a building that looks like a dungeon on the outside and a rabbit warren inside. During Tokyo's humid summer they are even more astonished to discover a complete lack of air-conditioning. Officials toil in sweat-soaked shirtsleeves in overcrowded offices at desks piled high with papers. Everything is done manually because there are virtually no computers. The finance ministry seemingly has no interest in electronic data, again in stark contrast to the high-tech ambience of central Tokyo, which has as good a claim as any of its global competitors to merit the title of tomorrow's city.

New entrants to this bizarre world are expected to work hard for a pittance. The starting salary is as low as ¥150,000 a month plus basic housing. In their first five years all manner of grunt work is thrust upon these young officials, and they are expected to work late into the night. Sleeping bunks are provided on the premises. Yet by the time an employee reaches the age of forty or achieves the *kacho* (section chief) level it would be considered quite improper for him to be seen in the finance ministry after 6:00 P.M. It would be interpreted as a sure sign that he was not having dinner with important people, be they from the world of politics, business, or finance, and that he therefore lacked influence. This is the ultimate sin. Bureaucrats who lack influence do not get good sinecures when they retire, at age fifty-five, in the process that is known as *amakudari*. The Ministry of Finance, as befits its prestige, is viewed as the best place for *amakudari*. Retiring finance ministry officials will go on to run quasi-government entities like the Japan Development Bank, the Export Bank, or even the Bank of Japan. Others will go to comfortable positions in organizations they formerly regulated—banks, insurance companies, or securities firms. Still others will go into politics. The world of officialdom and politics is not quite as separate as is suggested by the bureaucracy's image of itself as a mandarin elite standing aloof from the scheming graft-stained politicians. About one-third of the LDP members in the Diet are former Ministry of Finance officials. Relations between the finance ministry and the LDP are close to the point of intimacy, naturally so because of the web of personal ties that range "from the mutually supportive to the truly symbiotic," to quote from Karel van Wolferen's *The Enigma of Japanese Power*.

Traditionally, finance ministry officials used to leave the bureaucracy and enter politics when they were about fifty years old, when they were a spent force in terms of their careers as public servants. Miyazawa, the current prime minister, was the first finance ministry official to leave at the *kacho* level, when he was about thirty-five years old. Now more and more younger officials with political ambitions are leaving earlier so they will have more time to build a power base in the LDP. In keeping with the way the system works these pushy types will more often than not be married to the daughters of LDP figures. The result is an emerging generation of technocratic politicians, of whom Miyazawa is a pioneering example. Their differences with the more grass-roots politicians are clear from the arguments within the LDP over electoral reform, the issue that precipitated Kaifu's downfall in November 1991.

The published report of the Electoral Reform Commission was radical for Japan. They proposed creating 300 new single-seat constituencies for the lower house of the Diet. Another 171 members would be elected by proportional representation. Each voter would be able to cast two votes, one to pick a candidate for the local constituency and the other to select a party through proportional representation. This reform would have represented the most far-reaching change since the establishment of Japan's post-1945 political order. The LDP is divided between those in favor, who tend to be from under-represented urban constituencies, and those against, who tend to be populist types from the rural areas who want to continue with business as usual—traditional pork-barrel Japanese politics.

Although electoral reform did not pass in 1991 and even triggered Kaifu's downfall, the issue is bound to return. It is popular with the electorate, a fact that though not as important in Japan as in other democracies is not as completely irrelevant as cynics would suggest. It is apparent that the Japanese political system at some point has to start doing a better job of representing the urban voter, if only for the practical reason that this group accounts for a growing proportion of the population. The ambitious finance ministry officials who are moving at a younger age into politics will tend to be in favor of electoral reform and will naturally be more inclined toward representing the interests of the urban middle class. In this sense the potential exists for the nexus between the finance ministry and the political world to grow even more pronounced than it is already, perhaps prompting the creation of a new party should the LDP split up over a landmark constitutional issue such as electoral reform.

This is the political arena in which the Ministry of Finance holds a formidably powerful position. But in the world of finance, its own proprietary turf, the ministry now finds itself on an altogether more slippery slope. For unlike the introspective tribal world of Japanese politics, Japanese finance was buffeted during the 1980s both by self-induced shocks, such as the deregulation of interest rates, and unavoidable upheavals, such as the globalization of world financial markets and the free flow of investment capital. "Globalization" may have become an overused cliché during the booming 1980s, the word on the tip of the tongue of every young investment banker or management consultant who passed through business school. But for the Ministry of Finance this powerful trend did provide a source of acute discomfort. The more foreign banks and securities companies lobbied to be allowed to do more business in Japan, often with the active support of their political leaders, the more this international interest highlighted the anachronisms and rigidities of Japan's financial system at a time when Japan's domestic financial markets and financial industries required drastic change if they were to remain internationally competitive.

The antiquated nature of the Ministry of Finance was well described by Kenichi Ohmae, senior partner of McKinsey's Tokyo office, in an article he published in the *Asian Wall Street Journal* at the peak of the scandals. He wrote, "The Ministry of Finance is a dinosaur, designed for a time when Japan's financial industries were young and were believed to need protection and encouragement." Ohmae recommended that the overbearing ministry be broken up by function into several distinct units. This makes sense, just as it is sensible to dismantle unwieldy business conglomerates that lack internal synergies. The Ministry of Finance is indeed a dinosaur, the sprawling part-regulatory, part-enforcement agency that Ohmae describes. Its responsibilities cover the equivalent of several U.S. federal departments and agencies. The ministry draws up the national budget, as does the Office of Management and Budget and Congress, and manages the national debt, as does the United States Treasury. It collects taxes, as does the Internal Revenue Service. It is responsible for monitoring the condition and activities of financial firms, be they securities companies (the responsibility of the Securities and Exchange Commission in America), banks (the Office of the Comptroller of the Currency and the Federal Deposit Insurance Corporation), or insurance companies (state insurance regulators). Japan's all-embracing approach asks too much of a single institution. The sensible reform would be to convert the ministry's separate units, be it the tax bureau, the budget bureau, the securities bureau, or the banking bureau, into independent entities. The aim would be to stop the banking and securities units from viewing themselves as defenders of the turf interests of the providers of financial services, which is their traditional mentality and not unconnected with the fact that many of the officials plan to end up working in the industries they have spent a career regulating. Their purpose rather should be to protect the users of financial services, be they consumers or investors.

The too-cozy relationship between regulator and the regulated became obvious with the disclosure of the securities scandals. These revelations exposed the Ministry of Finance to unprecedented levels of public criticism, putting it on the defensive for the first time in its modern history. It began to dawn on people that "administrative guidance," the much-vaunted system whereby Japanese bureaucrats tell people what to do orally, not by written instruction, was in reality simply a means of granting the bureaucracy excessive license, of allowing officialdom to do what it wants to do. When there are no written rules there is no accountability. There is also great flexibility. Rules can be changed, or at least reinterpreted, whenever circumstances warrant.

Because loss compensation was the financial scandal that most exercised the average Japanese, the clamor for reform centered on the securities bureau. There were widespread calls for creation of an independent regulator on the model of America's SEC. The pressure was such that the ministry felt it had to respond. On September 13, 1991, the conclusions of a blue-ribbon committee on financial reform were made public. This body had been studying the issue of financial reform in general, in terms of deregulation and the breaking down of barriers between banking and brokering. But when the scandals erupted its mission was broadened to include the job of overhauling the finance ministry itself. The committee's proposal hardly did that. It recommended creation of a semi-independent watchdog called the Securities and Financial Inspection Commission, with the power to oversee Japan's financial markets. The commission was partly flying a kite. As usual, the details remained murky because a consensus had yet to be reached. There clearly would be constraints on the new body's independence. The new commission will report to the finance ministry. Its members will be appointed by the finance ministry. And the authority to punish will remain with the finance ministry. All this suggests that the finance ministry has prevailed with its argument that a fully independent American-style regulatory commission would be "unsuited" to Japan. The ministry's ability to fend off criticism of this half-measure reflected the remarkable tendency among Tokyo's financial groupies, long used to cultivating finance ministry officials, still to credit them with supernatural powers to prop up stock and property markets even after those markets had crashed. Such people seemed unable to conceive of existence without the overweening presence of the finance ministry.

The fact remains that even the committee's diluted reform is a big step for Japan, for some form of securities regulator will be set up. Before the scandals, a semi-independent watchdog patrolling the finance ministry's territory would have been unthinkable. Moreover, the committee's report calls for regulations to be codified and written down, a reform aimed at the ministry's nod-and-wink approach to regulation. The reforms should help to put more distance between regulator and regulated and is a first step toward a more legalistic system. The proposed watchdog will not be quite as toothless as scoffers suggest, assuming (a big if) the proposals are not weakened when finance ministry officials draft them. The commission will, for example, have the power to investigate banks and brokers and to confiscate documents. This should provide enough room for the watchdog to make a nuisance of itself should it so choose. At one point the ministry was not going to be allowed to appoint present or past officials to the new regulatory body. Unfortunately, there is a practical problem with this worthy goal.

Japan is woefully short of securities lawyers. There is, for example, no course taught in securities law in the University of Tokyo's law department. Indeed, the concept of ambitious young securities lawyers working as government prosecutors for a few years before moving to the private sector, as in the American tradition, is wholly alien to the Japanese system. This is why the finance ministry will be able to place many of its own men inside the regulatory body despite the commission's original good intentions. The best the securities regulator can probably hope for is that it achieves the same degree of independence as the tax agency, which is formally a part of the finance ministry but is independent in spirit and practice. It was, after all, the tax inspectors who triggered the loss-compensation scandal by taking exception to the brokers' cheeky attempts to write off their payments as business expenses.

This episode explains why there was great interest when a weekly magazine called *Themis* was abruptly closed down in July 1991 and had its last issue withdrawn hastily from the newsstands. That issue contained an article alleging that the information about the stockbrokers' compensation payments was leaked to the press nine days after Mamoru Ozaki became director general of the tax agency on June 11, which happens to be just about the time the scandal broke. Ozaki, whose nickname is said to be Devil Head because of his fearsome reputation as a tax collector, is a former boss of the agency's tax collection section. By contrast, his predecessor as director general, Masahiko Kadotani, was a former head of the finance ministry's securities bureau. It is most unusual in Japan for publications to be closed down as a result of such blatant government pressure. Perhaps Gakushu Kenkyusha, the publishing company that owned *Themis*, feared a tax audit.

Certainly, Ozaki's arrival coincided with stepped-up enforcement against tax dodgers. In this sense the debris from Japan's burst bubble has exposed not only scandal and fraud but also large-scale tax evasion. The numbers are huge. Consider the following examples. On October 1, 1991, public prosecutors asked for a three-year prison sentence for Toshiyuki Inamura, a former LDP Diet member and former director general of Japan's Environment

Agency. He was charged with evading some ¥1.7 billion in tax due from lucrative share-dealing profits. Inamura was an associate of Mitsuhiro Kotani, the former big-time stock market speculator who was facing securities and extortion charges. Kotani had been singing like a bird to prosecutors in an effort to secure more lenient treatment. He also squealed on Hirotomo Takei, the seventy-year-old former chairman of Chisan, a leisure and property company. Takei pleaded guilty in September to tax evasion totaling ¥3.4 billion, then the largest such case involving an individual. This case provided a glimpse into a side of Japanese commerce not taught at American business schools. Prosecutors told the court that Kotani had borrowed nearly ¥100 billion from the Chisan group. Faced with a repayment deadline that he was unable to meet, he sought to put pressure on Takei to delay repayment by telling a group of professional extortionists posing as right-wing activists that Takei had cheated on his taxes. This information was duly broadcast through loudspeakers outside Chisan's Tokyo head office (such a spectacle is a common sight in the streets of central Tokyo). Prosecutors said that in response Takei paid a *yakuza* gang ¥400 million to put an end to this noisy harassment. The tax authorities even extended their energies beyond politicians and the wheeler-dealers of the Bubble Economy to the great and the good. Earlier in 1991, Tadao Yoshia, president of YKK, the world's largest maker of zippers and a prominent establishment industrialist and philanthropist, was publicly identified as having failed to report ¥15 billion in taxable income. As a result, he had to pay an extra ¥3.3 billion in taxes on top of the ¥2.4 billion he had already forked out to meet the previous year's tax bill.

The tax men are prepared to flex their muscles independently of the rest of the Ministry of Finance. Theirs is an example the new securities regulator should aim to follow. It will help that at least its executive head will probably be selected from outside the finance ministry. The political judgment is that the public will demand a certain modicum of independence for the new regulatory body and will not accept a finance ministry appointee.

Further proof was soon to emerge that the finance ministry's authority had been damaged by the summer scandals on a more than temporary basis. The "best and the brightest" were clearly on the defensive. Ever since the scandals had exposed the inadequacies of their own "administrative guidance" in supervising the market, officials had been seeking to fend off not only pressure for a truly independent securities regulator but also a challenge to their whole method of operation. Administrative guidance itself was under attack. Foreign critics especially were demanding greater transparency in regulations so they could be sure that Japan was playing by the rules. Meanwhile, Nomura was off in a sulk because it felt it had been betrayed by officialdom that summer. The firm only showed up at the finance ministry when it had to and was playing no part in discussions about the makeup of the new securities regulator. This left a gaping vacuum for the bureaucrats at the securities bureau who were accustomed to leaning heavily on Nomura for practical advice when it came to drawing up regulations and the like. Just how big the vacuum was, and how badly Nomura's counsel was missed, became clear to the heads of foreign securities firms in Tokyo when they were summoned to a lunch hosted by the Japan Securities Dealers Association (JSDA) in December 1991. The purpose of the occasion was to brief them on a half-inch-thick document containing new "voluntary guidelines" to stop firms compensating clients for investment losses. The rules were voluntary because they were officially the rules of the JSDA, a self-regulating organization under the aegis of the finance ministry. They had been prepared because compensation would become a criminal offense in Japan on April 1, 1992, as a direct result of the scandals.

Drawing up guidelines seemed a sensible way to avoid confusion. But what amazed the foreign securities firms was that, however well intentioned, the bureaucrats were coming up with rules that were often hopelessly impractical and that revealed their ignorance about the way financial markets work. An example was a rule that stated that no more than 10,000 shares of any new issue could be placed with any one investor. Yet clearly a major institutional investor like Nippon Life, Japan's largest institutional investor, will want to purchase more than 10,000 shares in any issue it decides to buy. This may seem a trivial detail, but it is revealing since it shows what can go wrong if officials do not consult those in the business when they draw up rules. Now that the ministry is trying to show its independence and Nomura is brooding, the danger is that there is no communication between them at all. Clearly there will be attempts at dialogue like the old days, especially if the Nikkei index falls below the 20,000 level. At that point a sense of self-preservation will take over and there will likely be hastily prepared emergency measures announced in an attempt to prevent panic. The problem for Nomura, the finance ministry, and the stock market is that trust is a hard commodity to replace once lost.

The Ministry of Finance has had to suffer fresh insults to its reputation from an unexpected quarter: Japan's Fair Trade Commission (FTC), a body whose existence many in the securities business had probably forgotten about. The widespread disparagement of the FTC clearly rankled those who worked for it. In an interview in early 1992 with the author Akio Yamada, a director of the FTC and a noticeably less arrogant fellow than most of his bureaucratic counterparts at the Ministry of Finance, he recalled that a few years previously The Economist had described the FTC as "the watchdog that never bites." It is a description that is no longer valid. In late 1991 the FTC surprised itself and many others by displaying a new aggression. It documented for the first time how the Tokyo stock market was rigged by Japan's leading securities firms. This was the result of an investigation launched by the FTC in September (immediately after the finance ministry had completed its own halfhearted inquiries) into the loss-compensation scandal. It was the first such probe of the securities companies since the FTC was established in 1947 by the American occupation forces. The peculiarly American concept of antitrust was therefore grafted on to the Japanese system, much as a Japanese SEC was in 1948. But the finance ministry had the latter institution abolished in 1951 soon after the Americans departed, absorbing the commission's powers itself. The Japanese SEC was seen as a dangerously alien and therefore subversive influence. The finance ministry did not bother abolishing the FTC, a decision or an act of neglect it doubtless now regrets.

The results of the FTC's investigation became clear in late November when it issued one decree against each of the Big Four securities firms—Nomura, Daiwa, Nikko, and Yamaichi. The results showed up the Ministry of Finance. The decrees confirmed that all four firms had paid secret compensation to make up for losses or to produce guaranteed returns. The decrees ordered each firm to inform its officers, directors, employees, and clients that they had violated Japan's Antimonopoly Act and to promise that they would not commit such acts again. The securities companies had the option of either challenging these decrees in court or accepting them in writing. In early December they all signed legally binding consent decrees admitting their guilt. As a result, similar acts in future will lead to criminal sanctions, regardless of motive, according to Yamada.

The FTC's action is important for two reasons. It is a rare concession to transparency, which will please foreign lobbyists. It is also a sign that the Ministry of Finance is no longer all-powerful. The ministry was furious at what it saw as the FTC's infringement on its territory. It had regarded the summer's scandals as settled, and it certainly claimed responsibility for dealing with them. The FTC barged in by arguing that the scandals were an offense against fair trading, since brokers who abstained from compensating clients had been put at a competitive disadvantage.

The finance ministry may continue to lose turf, for the FTC's decrees also rammed home the message that the ministry's traditional style of regulation is no longer effective. The nods and winks of administrative guidance arguably contributed to the scandals. The FTC confirmed how in December 1989 the securities firms received two directives from the head of the finance ministry's securities bureau. The first said to stop compensating investors. The second said to wind up the *eigyo tokkin* accounts. The difficulty, as described earlier, was that these directives proved hard to implement in tandem once the stock market had begun, three months later, its steep descent. Many of the *eigyo tokkin* accounts were by then already under water. The only practical way to wind them up short of reneging on the guarantees given to investors was to generate phony profits by means of artificial trades. The FTC's decree records how Nomura's senior executive directors decided to continue indemnifying certain important clients at a meeting held on March 13, 1990, some three months after the finance ministry's directives.

The FTC's decrees also established for the first time that loss compensation was paid not only to get *eigyo tokkin* business, but to win underwriting business as well. The Ministry of Finance had said nothing about this aspect of the affair. Yamaichi, the weakest of the Big Four and a firm plagued in the final months of 1991 by perennial rumors of financial problems, paid the most in compensation, probably because it was the most desperate for business. The FTC report concluded that between October 1987 and the end of March 1991 Nomura paid ¥27.9 billion in compensation to fifty-two clients, Daiwa ¥24.5 billion to seventy-seven clients, Nikko ¥56.6 billion to eighty-three clients, and Yamaichi ¥62 billion to seventy-eight clients. The result of the FTC's investigation makes the Big Four more vulnerable to litigation, for they have now admitted that they did indeed commit criminal offenses. Consequently, litigants will only be required to prove damages. The Tokyo office of Coudert Brothers, a major American law firm, says it has several clients, including American mutual funds and pension funds, that are contemplating legal suits in America. They hope to claim back brokering commissions paid to the Big Four, fees paid to their investment-management affiliates, and even investment losses suffered in the Tokyo stock market. The FTC's decrees also came in handy for America's SEC, which by the time of the decrees' publication had already spent nearly six months looking informally into the American activities of the Big Four. Although no official SEC investigation had yet been announced, the Japanese brokers had been made to hand over piles of paper to the federal snoops in Washington.

The FTC's newfound zeal did not end with these decrees. In another case launched almost simultaneously the commission appeared to attack a convention that Japan's ruling establishment, in particular the Ministry of Finance, had long tolerated by turning a blind eye. It related to cross-shareholdings, the warp and woof of the Japanese economy. Companies take stakes in one another not for investment purposes but as a way of consolidating business relationships and doing mutual favors. A law forbids financial firms from owning more than 5 percent of another company, but nobody has expected more than the letter of this law to be observed. That was true until September 1991 when the FTC suddenly decided to investigate the tie between Nomura Securities and Nomura Land and Building. The securities firm formally owns only 5 percent of the property-holding company. Nomura Land and Building's main reason for existence is to manage the properties owned by Nomura Securities in Japan, including its branch network. But it also owns 50 percent of Nomura Real Estate, a property-development company that reported revenues of some ¥150 billion in the year ending March 1991.

The FTC discovered that in the 1960s individual owners had transferred shares in Nomura Land and Building to three companies: Sanwa Bank; Obayashi Corporation, a construction firm; and Asahi Fire and Marine, a property and casualty insurance company. Nomura Securities drew up memoranda with each of these companies that imposed two key restrictions. The first was that the shares could not be sold without Nomura's approval; the second, that Nomura retained the right to buy the shares back at the original purchase price. Nomura Securities concluded a similar agreement with Nomura Research Institute (NRI), another nominally independent entity, when another ten individual shareholders transferred their Nomura Land and Building shares to NRI between 1987 and 1989.

The FTC issued its decree in November 1991. It ordered these agreements to be torn up and all restrictions lifted on the sale of the shares. Nomura accepted this judgment by again signing a legally binding consent decree. Still, the securities firm must have felt that it had been singled out. It seems more than a coincidence that the FTC suddenly pursued this case just a few months after the disclosure of the securities scandals in which Nomura was the most prominent offender. Other brokers and banks are likely to have similar arrangements in place with friendly shareholders, though at least in the banks' case they may not be quite as crudely structured as Nomura's memos. The Long-Term Credit Bank only owns 5 percent of its property affiliate Nippon Landic but, as described earlier, was somehow able to persuade the company to buy its headquarters building in 1991 for substantially more than the market price. The Industrial Bank of Japan (IBJ) formally owns only 5 percent of New Japan Securities, but the securities firm is considered IBJ's brokering affiliate.

If the FTC were to apply the logic of the Nomura case to every important financial firm in Japan, and so start untying the knots of cross-shareholdings, it would risk destruction of the whole financial fabric, which is why this is most unlikely to happen. Meanwhile, Sanwa Bank, Obayashi Corporation, and Asahi Fire and Marine could make a pile of money by selling their Nomura Land and Building shares. However dramatic the recent fall in property prices, the shares are still bound to be worth more than they were some twenty-five years ago. Whether these shareholders would dare, or would even want, to risk Nomura's ire by reneging on the spirit of their agreement by selling out is another matter.

The Ministry of Finance was infuriated by the FTC's chipping away at long-standing conventions. Finance ministry officials look down on the commission's officials. They say there are only about ten competent people working at the FTC and they no doubt are former finance ministry men. Another reason they disdain the FTC is because there is often no job in the private sector for its officials when they retire from the government. In the warped logic of Kasumigaseki, there is no point in working in such a place. *Amakudari* does not apply to the FTC because Japanese companies do not think they need to worry about the enforcement of antitrust laws. Therefore, they do not perceive a need to employ specialists in this area. The irony is that the more aggressive the FTC becomes, the more the services of its retired officials will be sought by the private sector. This is a useful example of the rule that in

Japan respect is only accorded to strength. The Ministry of Finance also worried that the FTC's new aggression would make it harder for the ministry to make policy. Its preferred way of working is to get the leaders of the top business groups together in a room, be they the chairmen of the city banks or the heads of the Big Four, and hammer out a consensus. Was it possible that the FTC would now consider such meetings violations of antitrust regulations? The technical answer to this is no, so long as prices or market shares are not fixed. The practical problem is that such meetings are easily open to misinterpretation because relations between the Ministry of Finance and the banks and brokers have tended to be highly informal and personal. This is why the postscandal feud between Nomura and the finance ministry has the quality of a falling-out between friends. It is also why the Ministry of Finance was lobbying at the end of 1991 for one of its own to take over the FTC when the post of chairman came up for renewal in September 1992. The current chairman, Setsui Umezewa, is a former head of the tax agency who will have been in the post for five years. The Ministry of Finance wants Masami Kogayu to replace him. Kogayu served in the finance ministry's top post of administrative vice-minister until June 1991. That it wants to get one of its most senior career bureaucrats appointed to run the FTC indicates the extent to which the Ministry of Finance feels its traditional tool of control, administrative guidance, is threatened by the FTC's actions.

The Ministry of Finance's authority may have been diminished both within the narrow world of Kasumigaseki and throughout the country at large by the criticisms directed at it as a result of the scandals. After all, the Bubble Economy occurred on its watch. However, if its reputation has been tainted somewhat, it still remains the most powerful government ministry, its position sealed by its budgetary role and its tight, almost symbiotic, relationship with the ruling LDP. For that reality to change would require a breakup of the post-1945 political order and, more specifically, the end of LDP rule. The lesson of the Recruit scandal is that the LDP is likely to survive anything thrown at it in the way of scandalous disclosures and resignations of prime ministers so long as it continues to deliver the goods economically. As this book was being finished, the political world was full of talk of a scandal that it was said would make Recruit look like a sideshow. The scandal centered on political contributions paid by the Tokyo subsidiary of a Kyoto-based transport company called Sagawa Kyubin, which is Japan's second-largest parcel-delivery company, with annual sales in 1990 of ¥810 billion. At the center of the widely discussed but (in a curious example of press self-censorship) little-publicized affair was the existence of a document allegedly written by Hiroyasu Watanabe, the president of the company's Tokyo subsidiary, listing two hundred LDP and opposition party politicians who had received funds totaling more than ¥50 billion. Five former prime ministers were said to be on the list. In addition to the issue of political graft, the Tokyo Sagawa Kyubin affair also has bubble overtones. Watanabe was dismissed from the company in July 1991 after the discovery of financial scams and was subsequently charged with extraordinary breach of trust. He is said to have provided more than ¥500 billion in loans and loan guarantees to forty different companies, of which ¥100 billion ended up with companies controlled by or linked to the Inagawa-kai, the *yakuza* syndicate. Many of these loans were made to paper companies set up solely to obtain bank financing and controlled by the late Susumu Ishii, the former chairman of the Inagawa-kai who had featured in the securities scandals. The sheer scale of these fraudulent loan guarantees has now landed Sagawa Kyubin in serious financial difficulties, which has given the police the cause to investigate. The Tokyo subsidiary, with annual sales of ¥160 billion, is already in receivership with some ¥200 billion of debts. In February Tokyo police raided twenty-three sites, including Watanabe's home and the offices of the Inagawa-kai, in connection with investigations into the case.

The extent to which this particular scandal causes problems for the LDP, and so for the stock market, is impossible to say, although more arrests seem bound to occur. The word in Nagatacho, Tokyo's political district, is that it is not so great a problem because virtually everyone was on the take, including the opposition parties, with the exception of the communists. This would be a correct judgment in normal times, though it should also be noted that a similar sort of we-are-all-in-it-together logic was used to justify buying Japanese shares when the Nikkei index was at nearly 39,000. However, if the economy stops delivering the goods it must be wondered the extent to which the political order can withstand the seemingly constant revelation of scandal that has become common in recent years. There is plenty of evidence that the Japanese people are fed up if not plain disgusted with their politicians. The popularity of Kaifu, a pigmy in LDP power-politics terms but a man respected by the electorate for his relatively clean image, is an example. It is therefore clear that the political and bureaucratic establishment's sole claim to legitimacy rests on its record of economic management. The land boom frayed the social consensus. But the bust of the Bubble Economy raises the threat of the sort of deflationary economic downturn that could cause a shattering of confidence in the ruling order and the consequent disintegration of a political system that increasingly exhibits all the signs of paralysis.

# 9

# The Economy

In early 1991 a timely booklet was published by the Jerome Levy Economics Institute of Chappaqua, New York. It was titled "Outlook for the 1990s: The Contained Depression." The thrust of the paper was directed at the American economy. But its central argument could be applied to the rest of the world economy, nowhere more so than in Japan.

The paper's thesis was that the world economy was suffering from having too many of the wrong assets built at the wrong time at excessive prices and paid for with too much debt. It also theorized that the debt excesses of the 1980s would lead to deflation in the 1990s, not inflation. The study went on to describe how monetary policy would not by itself be able to restart a depressed economy suffering from asset deflation and widespread financial crisis, for "lower interest rates cannot motivate fixed investment when the market is glutted with existing assets worth much less than it costs to replace them." The result would be that central bankers would be left "pushing on a string," to borrow the famously graphic phrase coined earlier this century by British economist John Maynard Keynes.

The argument that unprecedented levels of debt would render central banks and conventional monetary policy ineffective in the next economic downturn because lenders would be too scared to lend and borrowers too scared to borrow has been described fully before.* The Levy Institute's booklet was a welcome sign that a few conventional economists were finally beginning to comprehend the deflationary forces that are at work in the early 1990s and to understand that the post-1945 conventional wisdom taught to millions of undergraduates, namely that central banks could cure all economic pain by the simple expedient of cutting interest rates, is among the most dangerous of modern myths. It has encouraged extreme complacency on the part of those willing to dig themselves ever deeper into debt, comforted by the assumptions that slumps and falling prices are relics of economic history and that inflation will always be on hand to bail out borrowers.

By the end of 1991 the limited possibilities of monetary policy in a deflationary downturn were painfully obvious to millions of ordinary Americans and even to some economists. The same message was also beginning to dawn on an increasingly concerned business community in Japan, even if the Bank of Japan itself had not yet quite gotten the message, so determined was it to kill the country's speculative bubble for good. In December America's Federal Reserve signaled its own growing alarm when it unexpectedly cut the discount rate by a full percentage point to its lowest level in twenty-eight years. Alan Greenspan, chairman of the Federal Reserve, made his concerns crystal clear when he testified before Congress on December 19, the day before this dramatic move, that never in his career had he witnessed such a collapse in consumer confidence. He told the assembled legislators, "There is a deep-seated concern out there which I admit I have not seen in my lifetime." This was powerful language for a naturally cautious central banker, a breed who always weigh their words with particular care. It did not take long for the quickening pace of central bank easing to spread across the Pacific. On the second to last day of 1991 the Bank of Japan in a surprise move also cut its official

---

*Boom and Bust: The Rise and Fall of World Financial Markets. Sidgwick and Jackson 1988; Atheneum 1989.

discount rate for the third time that year. The move was made only a matter of days before American president George Bush was due to arrive in Tokyo on his ill-fated visit ostensibly to push for more American imports into Japan but also to lobby for Japanese action to stimulate the world economy. Because of these mounting political pressures, Bank of Japan officials were anxious at the time not to appear to have been panicked into easing. Instead, they portrayed the move as part of a gradualist transition to an easier monetary policy. The central bank still claimed not to be worried by signs of a sharply slowing Japanese economy, an illiquid and weakening property market, and a beleaguered stock market, arguing that these were all just part of a normal process of adjustment following a period of excessively fast economic growth. Yet this posture of official calm was becoming harder to maintain. In private, central bank officials conceded that one set of statistics— monetary growth—was not behaving as it was supposed to. The Bank of Japan had been easing monetary policy since the late spring of 1991, yet growth in the money supply in the year ending January 1992 hit a record low on each of its two main measures. Short-term interest rates had collapsed by more than three percentage points from over 8 percent in the spring of 1991 to 5 percent by early 1992, but monetary growth had not yet picked up as expected, despite a Bank of Japan prediction back in June that money supply growth had then reached its low point. With a weakening economy, falling inflation, and stagnating monetary growth, it was no wonder the central bank was facing mounting pressure to ease.

This slower than expected monetary growth was no coincidence. This was exactly the same pattern that preceded America's recession, which formally began in the summer of 1990. It is a useful rule of thumb that in this economic cycle Japan has been about a year to eighteen months behind America. American monetary growth was weak long before its economy formally entered recession. The cause was slowing loan growth (not a restrictive central bank) as deflationary forces caused by excessive levels of debt gradually overwhelmed individuals' desire to take on still more debt. This led to a change in behavior. The year 1991 marked the first time in a generation that American companies and consumers decided to get out of debt. Consumer debt actually contracted. Slowing loan growth, and the resulting lackluster monetary growth, was a portent of what was to come. For total debt contraction, or even a drastic slowdown in the growth of debt, is deflationary. America's experience provided the clue as to why the money supply was not growing as fast as the Bank of Japan thought it should in the second half of 1991. There were two principal causes. First, Japan's undercapitalized banks were reluctant to lend. Bank lending barely kept up with inflation in 1991. Bankers were cautious because they were uncomfortably aware of their mounting burden of bad property loans, even if they were not admitting them in public. Banks also needed to trim their balance sheets to meet the BIS international capital adequacy standards. The second reason for slowing monetary growth was that companies were suddenly not so keen on borrowing. Corporate profits fell in 1991 as the Japanese economy slowed, while companies' cost of capital rose alarmingly. Investors were no longer willing to pay premium prices for equity-linked securities, such as bonds with warrants, which Japanese companies had been able to issue with abandon in the boom years because of the soaring Tokyo stock market. Instead, Japanese companies were opting to run down their holdings of cash and short-term securities. Their net liquid assets (cash, bank deposits, and short-term securities) fell by ¥8.9 trillion in the second quarter of 1991, a record quarterly decline.

A key point to watch will be how long it takes for monetary growth to respond to central bank easing. The American record is not very encouraging. The Federal Reserve lowered the federal funds rate from 10 percent in the spring of 1989 to 3 percent at the end of 1990 with little effect on monetary growth. In Japan the third official discount rate cut in December 1991 indicated mounting official alarm. Japan has more reason to worry about this deflationary undertow than most of its economists and policymakers realize. The reason why is contained in a useful distinction put forward by the Levy Institute as to the difference between a recession and a depression: "Recessions are retrenchments necessitated by overproduction; depressions are caused by overinvestment. The primary imbalances in a recession are inventories; in a depression, they are in structures and capacity. Inventory imbalances can be corrected quickly; excess structures and capacity take years to absorb."

This distinction is peculiarly important to Japan. In the late 1980s Japan kept expanding its industrial capacity "as if it were still in the midst of a transition from small, developing economy to leading industrial power and had prospects of rapidly expanding its trade surplus," to quote the Levy Institute. In fact, Japan was by then a mature, established economy, the world's second largest, whose consistently high trade surplus had long exhausted the patience of most of its trading partners, a fact to which Bush's politically charged January 1992 visit was a testament. Yet corporate Japan indulged in what can only be described as investment overkill in the late 1980s. Japanese companies embarked on the biggest capital-spending spree in the country's postwar history. Fueled by superlow interest rates and a soaring stock market, capital spending became more than ever the virility symbol of Japan's economy. It accounted for two-thirds of the growth in GNP between late 1986 and early 1991, the duration of the so-called *Heisei* expansion. During this time Japan's net new investment amounted to a staggering $3.5 trillion. Deutsche Bank's Tokyo-based economist, Kenneth Courtis, has put this spending in some context. Primarily as a result of all this private business investment the Japanese economy expanded by the equivalent of South Korea's GNP each year of the *Heisei* boom and at the end of it was "one France larger" than it was just five years earlier. The Japanese economy is now twice the size of Germany and (based on its recent frantic growth rate) is doubling in size every fifteen years, according to Courtis.

The very scale of this capital spending makes the Japanese economy peculiarly vulnerable to any sudden fall in business investment. At the end of 1991 capital spending represented 23 percent of Japan's gross national product. A 10 percent decline in capital spending would of itself reduce real GNP growth by over two percentage points. This is precisely what is now about to occur. It would be nice to think that Japanese companies' formidable capital spending plans were solely explained by technological innovation and Japanese industry's much-lauded ability to plan ahead. They were certainly a factor. But the incredibly low cost of money played an even bigger part. Japanese companies felt that they had to spend money since it seemed to cost them so little to raise it. Between 1985 and 1990 Japanese companies raised some ¥85 trillion through seemingly free equity-related financings. Conventional wisdom has it that most of this money (when it did not go into *tokkin* funds to play *zaitech* games in the stock market) went into building new productive capacity or into investing in technological innovation and research and development. Although most of the funds were nominally poured into these areas—Courtis guesses that some $3 trillion was invested in new domestic plants and capital equipment and $500 billion in research and development—anecdotal evidence and common sense suggest that a significant proportion was spent wastefully. When money seems free it is likely to be spent a good deal more lavishly than when its cost is prohibitive. Examples of wasteful Japanese investment range from fancy new headquarters buildings and brand-new laboratories without the qualified staff to fill them to spending on every sort of staff amenity—shiny new corporate dormitories for employees, swimming pools, saunas, and so forth.

This latter sort of spending on staff facilities was rationalized, like most other capital spending, by rising concerns about a worsening shortage of labor in Japan. The theory was that since people could not afford to buy their own homes because of Japan's land price bubble (itself a consequence of cheap money and arcane regulations) companies that wanted to attract the best employees and keep them had to offer housing and other facilities. This meant companies buying costly land during the bubble years either to build such facilities on it or simply for speculative purposes. In fiscal 1989, for example, Japanese companies spent ¥13.5 trillion buying land. Yet land purchases are not included in the official government measure of a business's fixed investment, or capital spending, because land is not considered a reproducible asset. This means that companies' investment spending was even greater than government statistics suggest. It was clearly absurd for Japanese companies to have been spending vast sums buying land at boom prices on which to build dormitories and the like, given both the long-term decline facing Japanese land prices and the dreary implications for the Japanese people's quality of life. An economy as rich as Japan's should not have its leading companies house junior and middle-ranking executives in dormitories far away from their homes and families. Such a state of affairs is as ludicrous as it is unsustainable.

In fact, Japan's much talked about labor shortage is a myth, as is the country's perceived land shortage. Both myths fail to take into account the distortions introduced by quirky regulations and arcane laws. They also underestimate the effect of the price mechanism at work, in the same way as 1970s's believers in a permanent energy shortage ignored the ability of the OPEC cartel to price itself out of the market. Just as the land shortage could be swiftly ended by reforming zoning laws and lowering capital gains taxes on the sale of property, so a reform of existing work practices would dramatically reduce the shortage of labor. This is not to say that Japan does not face a demographic problem; the number of people entering its work force will actually start falling in 1994. But this does not prove the fact of a labor shortage. In fact, there is tremendous waste in the way people are employed in Japan's service industries. Overstaffing is massive outside the manufacturing sector, which is the main reason why Japanese productivity per man-hour worked is still below America's despite all the rhetoric about American economic decline.

The Japanese economic miracle is therefore based to a dangerously narrow extent on the capital-intensive industrial sector. The capital spending spree of the late 1980s was a lopsided expression of this trend taken to its most logical extreme. Japanese manufacturers attempted to automate their way out of the perceived labor shortage while the country's service sector continued to wallow in an excess of labor. A survey conducted by Nippon Credit Bank in the summer of 1990 found that 91 percent of firms surveyed gave "rationalization" (measures to reduce labor costs) as the main reason for their capital spending that year, compared with only 42 percent that cited "capacity expansion" (the ability to make more goods). While companies fretted about the presumed shortage of workers, the same survey by Nippon Credit Bank found that 86 percent of the firms covered saw declines in the stock market as having only a negligible impact on their spending plans.

If these firms are wrong about the labor shortage they were also wrong about the stock market. Not even Japanese companies always plan correctly. Eighteen months later it was clear that much of that seemingly costless equity financing, which paid for the private investment boom, would not be free at all, since maturing bonds would have to be refinanced as warrants expired worthless. Corporate Japan's cost of capital had risen markedly. This financing crunch was forcing companies finally to revise down their capital spending plans. The crunch is likely to be a lot more serious than official Japan even now acknowledges. An early hint of the future came in August 1990 when Toshikatsu Fukama, chief financial officer at Mitsui and Company, a major trading company, went on the firm's intercom to deliver a timely message to the troops. He told them to discard attitudes that made sense only when interest rates were low. His message was that with market rates over 8 percent there was no point in presenting top management with business plans that still assumed the traditional target of a 5 percent return on capital employed. This episode revealed two things: First, that Mitsui's top brass thought it necessary to state what should have been obvious. It was necessary because Japanese managers for the past ten years had not had to think about financing costs. Second, that trading companies were likely to grasp the implications of dearer money more quickly than manufacturing companies. For as suppliers of investment capital and spotters of business opportunities, trading companies had to live off their wits. But by the end of 1991, as their interest bills climbed and their profits slumped, a growing number of manufacturing companies were waking up to the same reality.

The reason that capital spending will decline more severely than most conventional economists still expect is not only that Japanese industry has overinvested in a world economy that is slowing fast and has a monumental excess of productive capacity. It also is because Japanese companies themselves no longer have the money to fund such extravagance. Corporate Japan faces an unprecedented financing crunch. This was documented in a 1990 study by Kermit Schoenholtz, a then Tokyo-based economist for Salomon Brothers. Schoenholtz calculated, based on finance ministry quarterly statistics, that Japan's nonfinancial companies in fiscal 1990 faced a record financing gap of ¥61 trillion, or the equivalent of nearly 14 percent of GNP. This gap represents the difference between companies' cash flow and how much money they spend. Even excluding costly land acquisition, this financing gap still came to a record ¥47 trillion. The Salomon economist describes this shift of the corporate sector into a record-high net financial deficit as one of the most significant changes that has taken place in Japan's flow of funds in the past twenty-five years. He also notes that it is probably unsustainable because it is harder for companies to raise funds and, when they do, it is more expensive to borrow. As a result, companies have been using up their spare cash to maintain their levels of capital spending. This "liquidity drawdown," the ugly term economists use to describe companies' cash spending, totaled a record ¥7.3 trillion in the fiscal year ending March 1991. As already noted, it was even greater in the first three months of the 1991–92 financial year. Frittering away cash in this way is unsustainable over the longer term. It merely delays a trip to the bank or to the capital markets to borrow or postpones an already overdue cut in capital spending. With the banks reducing their lending and with capital more expensive, most of the impact is likely to be in the form of cuts in capital spending. Seeming confirmation of this trend came in a survey published by the *Nihon Keizai Shimbun* in February 1992. It projected an 11 percent decline in manufacturing investment in the fiscal year ending March 1993 and an overall 4.5 percent decline if nonmanufacturing companies are included. This was significantly worse than consensus forecasts. The *Nihon* survey made a December 1991 13.9 percent year-on-year decline in private machinery orders (described by Barclays De Zoete Wedd's Tokyo economist Peter Morgan as looking like "a jump off the cliff") appear all the more ominous.

The sheer scale of Japan's debt-based capital-spending cycle in the late 1980s makes it, not America, the most likely candidate to suffer the world's most wrenching debt deflation in the 1990s. "Debt deflation" was the term used by American Irving Fisher, a Yale economist, in an article written in 1933 at the nadir of the Great Depression. Fisher's paper, "The Debt Deflation Theory of Great Depressions," was revolutionary. It identified two stages on the road to depression. First, too-high levels of aggregate debt depress economic activity because of all the money spent servicing that debt (i.e., paying interest). Fisher termed this debt deflation. This is what America first, and now Japan, has suffered in their property markets as asset values have collapsed and debts have gone bad. Fisher argued that debt deflation only leads to general depression when there is a fall in the general price level. This has so far been avoided in the 1990s, though it is *the* big risk the world economy faces as a result of the bust of Japan's credit boom. Fisher wrote, "Just as a bad cold leads to pneumonia, so over-indebtedness leads to deflation."

The horror of a general fall in prices is the severe impact it has on the cost of borrowing and on the real amount of money owed. This requires some explanation. For where prices are falling by 10 percent annually, real interest rates (rates after inflation is taken into account) are 10 percent even if the nominal rate of interest is zero. The resulting deflationary dynamic as debts are liquidated is best described in the words of Fisher himself: "Deflation caused by the debt reacts on the debt. Each dollar of debt still unpaid becomes a bigger dollar, and if the over-indebtedness with which we started was great enough, the liquidation of debts cannot keep up with the fall of prices which it causes. In that case, the liquidation defeats itself. While it diminishes the number of dollars owed, it may not do so as fast as it increases the value of each dollar owed. Then,

*the every effort of individuals to lessen their burden of debts in-
creases it, because of the mass effect of the stampede to liquidate
in swelling each dollar owed.* Then we have the great paradox
which, I submit, is the chief secret of most, if not all, great depressions: *The more the debtors pay, the more they owe."*

Fisher's theory was important because it showed both that
debt matters and also how real interest rates can remain onerously
high even when nominal rates are practically zero. Conventional
economics teaches that debt does not matter because for every
debtor there is a corresponding creditor, and the two cancel each
other out. This cute academic theory explains most economists'
extraordinary lack of concern at the accumulation of debt during
the 1980s, which was on a far greater scale than anything witnessed in the 1920s. To most of them the buildup of debt during
this period was simply not an issue. Instead, they continued to be
obsessed about yesterday's problem, inflation. Unfortunately, this
view that debt does not matter only makes sense, as does a lot of
other economic hocus-pocus, when perfect equilibrium is assumed.
In this case, the assumption is that all debts are serviced on time.
But when debts go bad creditors get hurt, as money disappears and
the money supply contracts, just as it did in the 1930s. Such a
general fall in the price level is what central bankers are now trying
desperately to avoid. The increasingly visible fact of debt deflation
in the 1990s has finally made the more thoughtful among their
number realize that a repeat of the 1930s general fall in prices may
not be so impossible after all.

Japan's capital spending binge matters in this respect because
Fisher showed that the contractionary consequences are worse
when an excess of useful things, like factories, are produced. This
is for the simple reason that such worthy items do not need to be
replaced for a long time. Fisher's description of the possible origins
of overindebtedness also read like an up-to-date account of Japan's
bubble. "Easy money is the great cause of over-borrowing. When an
investor thinks he can make over 100 percent per annum by borrowing at 6 percent he will be tempted to borrow, and to invest or
speculate with borrowed money. This was a prime cause leading to

the over-indebtedness of 1929. Inventions and technical improve-
ments created wonderful investment opportunities, and so caused
big debts." Fisher's description of the changes in popular mood as
the fashion for debt grows also strikes a modern note. He wrote,
"The public psychology of going into debt for gain passes through
several more or less distinct phases: (a) the lure of big prospective
dividends or gains in income in the remote future; (b) the hope of
selling at a profit, and in realizing a capital gain in the immediate
future; (c) the vogue of reckless promotions, taking advantage of
the habituation of the public to great expectations; (d) the development of downright fraud, imposing on a public which had grown
credulous and gullible." The last instance shows that Japan's financial scandals, as a symptom of financial excess, are nothing
new. But as Fisher noted they are not the cause of the bust but
rather are the sort of detritus that can be confidently expected to
rise to the surface as a result of the bust. Some light on this trend
was also shed by Harvard economist John Kenneth Galbraith, in his
history of the 1929 Wall Street crash. His book reveals almost
uncanny similarities between contemporary Japanese finance and
the abuses that flourished on Wall Street during the 1920s but that
were only exposed fully after the crash. This is not so surprising,
since in terms of its historic development and general lack of
sophistication the Tokyo stock market in the 1980s had more in
common with the Wall Street of the 1920s than of the 1980s.
Galbraith wrote, "Just as the boom accelerated the rate of growth,
so the crash enormously advanced the rate of discovery. Within a
few days, something close to universal trust turned into something
akin to universal suspicion. Audits were ordered. Strained or preoccupied behavior was noticed. Most important the collapse in stock
values made irredeemable the position of the employee who had
embezzled to play the market. He now confessed." Galbraith also
pointed out how a long time could lapse between the commitment
of fraud and its subsequent discovery. During this period the fraud
helped keep the speculative fires burning. "Weeks, months, or
years may elapse between the commission of the crime and its
discovery. . . . At any given time there exists an inventory of

undiscovered embezzlement in—or more precisely not in—the country's business and banks. This inventory—it should perhaps be called the bezzle—amounts at any moment to many millions of dollars.'' But even Galbraith could scarcely have imagined the bezzle discovered in Japan's bust in the form of the billions of dollars worth of phony CDs that the banks provided to their clients.

These comparisons are made to illustrate the cyclical nature of Japan's speculative bust and the possibility that it portends another global slump into depression. Comparisons between the 1920s and 1930s and the 1980s and 1990s are easily ridiculed, but the fact is that there are too many similarities for cyclical theories about the ebb and flow of credit to be dismissed out of hand. Obviously, history never repeats itself exactly. But equally obviously, only a fool would choose to ignore it. Even if history does not repeat itself, it most certainly rhymes.

This is the largest of themes. But at the level of individual industries it is increasingly apparent that key industrial sectors of Japan's economy may have already installed all the productive capacity they really need for several years ahead. Take the automotive industry. Cars and car parts are the largest component of Japan's trade surplus with America. By 1993 the Japanese carmakers will have ten factories in America, all of which have been built in the past ten years. It is quite possible that no more will be built during the next ten years. Honda, for example, does not plan to build an assembly plant in America, Europe, or Japan until late in the 1990s. And Honda is usually a trendsetter for Japanese carmakers. It was, for example, the first Japanese carmaker to build a car plant in America. Japan's carmakers also face a glutted car market at home. Just about everybody who wants to own a car in Japan already has one. Sales will now stagnate both for demographic reasons and for reasons of physical constraint. Two-car families are a luxury in a country where a parking space costs some ¥60,000 a month and where proof of having an off-street parking space is required before purchase of a car.

Japan's other key industry, electronics, faces similar problems.

Sony, like Honda an innovator in its field, made headlines in early 1992 when it announced it would lose money in the year ending March 1992, its first loss ever. Sony also said it would cut capital spending for its forthcoming fiscal year by one-third, or ¥70 billion. Sony may have special problems because of the ¥1 trillion of debt it took on buying America's CBS Records in 1988 and Columbia Pictures in 1989. But its problems are not unique. Toshiba, NEC, and Fujitsu have all slashed their profit forecasts and announced major cuts in capital investment.

By the end of 1991 the signs of a rapidly slowing economy were becoming obvious. Yet many economists still clung to forecasts of 3 percent GNP growth for the fiscal year ending March 1993, and the official Economic Planning Agency to an even more optimistic 3.5 percent. This seemed increasingly bizarre given the evidence of weakness, which extended beyond capital spending. Growth in the money supply was feeble. Bank lending was almost flat. Housing starts and car sales were in steep declines. Industrial production in December was actually 1.9 percent lower than a year earlier. Workers' winter bonuses rose by only 3 percent, down from the previous year's 7 percent. Consumption, which accounts for 57 percent of GNP, was sluggish at best, with mounting evidence of something worse to come. Sales at Tokyo department stores declined by 2.4 percent year-on-year in December, the largest drop since 1965. Consumer electronics sales declined by 10 percent year-on-year in December as well. A few economists began to wonder if the lackluster trend in consumption reflected signs of a wealth effect taking hold as a result of the steep falls in the stock market and property market. There is some evidence for this in the form of a large gap that has opened up between employment income growth and consumption growth. Between January and September 1991, year-on-year growth of employment income averaged 5.5 percent, while consumption rose by only 2.8 percent. Barclays De Zoete Wedd's Morgan notes that such a large and prolonged gap is unprecedented in the past ten years.

Still, capital spending remains key. This is where the blow is likely to come that will have the most negative impact on the overall economy. It will take the form of at least two years of double-digit declines in private business investment. The importance of capital spending as a swing factor is highlighted by Susumu Saito, a Tokyo-based private economist. He calls it the "reverse multiplier effect." Saito notes that the ratio of private business investment to nominal GNP growth in Japan has fluctuated between 15 percent and 20 percent for the past thirty years. Within this pattern he has detected a trend. Once the ratio falls below 20 percent the growth rate of nominal GNP halves. It takes about four years for the ratio to decline to 15 percent. The latest boom generated maximum nominal GNP growth of only 7.65 percent in fiscal 1990. As of September 1991, nominal GNP was ¥456 trillion and capital spending was ¥89 trillion. If nominal GNP growth is 6 percent annually it will total ¥575 trillion in four years. If during that period the ratio of nominal GNP growth to capital spending falls to 15 percent, then business investment will total ¥86 trillion. But if nominal GNP growth drops to 4 percent annually and the ratio of nominal GNP to capital spending again drops to 15 percent, then capital spending will be an even lower ¥80 trillion, which is a 10 percent decline from current levels. This is hardly alarmist. Given its present rate of monetary growth of barely 2 percent, the Japanese economy will be lucky to achieve nominal GNP growth of even 4 percent. That sort of nominal growth would normally be expected by economists to require monetary growth in the 6 to 7 percent range.

So, as is already the case in America, Japanese economists, investors, and central bankers will be studying money-supply data more and more carefully and praying for a surge in monetary growth. They should not count on it. The debt-ravaged banking system does not have the capital to fund this sort of monetary expansion, and companies do not have the willingness to borrow. The latest monetary figures are certainly not auspicious. In January 1992 M2 plus certificates of deposit, the central bank's favorite measure of money supply, grew at an all-time low of 1.8 percent. Thus monetary growth, or the lack of it, poses a growing threat to economic growth. It also prompts mounting calls from businessmen and politicians for the Bank of Japan to cut interest rates aggressively, as America's Greenspan has done. In 1992, the LDP's political godfather Shin Kanemaru publicly called for an immediate half-a-percentage-point cut in the official discount rate.

At some point the Bank of Japan will have to give in more convincingly to these pressures. It is reluctant to do so because it is worried about the yen. This is why in early 1992 the central bank was busy trying to talk up the value of the yen as well as intervening in the foreign-exchange markets by selling dollars. Its efforts are likely to fail because it is bucking a fundamental trend. A weakening Japanese economy and the resulting expectations of lower interest rates, combined with a rush of political scandals, increase the risk of a falling yen. The usual reason given for why the Bank of Japan is so worried about the yen has to do with seeking to prevent trade frictions. The weaker the yen, the cheaper, and so more competitive, Japanese exports become and therefore the higher the trade surplus is likely to grow. However, there are two other equally important reasons for the Bank of Japan's concern about the currency. First, a weaker yen boosts inflationary pressures by raising the cost of buying dollar-denominated imported commodities such as oil. This in turn reduces the ability of the Bank of Japan to lower interest rates and so avert or at least reduce the impact of the banking crisis, the property crash, and the economic slowdown. Second, and perhaps more important, a weaker yen damages the banks' capital ratios. Because nearly 50 percent of the city banks' assets are denominated in foreign currencies (mainly dollars), the result of the maniacal overseas lending binge of the late 1980s, Japan's biggest banks are extremely vulnerable to a decline in the yen. For they have funded those loans, many of which are now in default, by borrowing dollars offshore in London's Euromarkets. The lower the yen falls, the more it will cost the banks to pay back those dollars and the worse the crisis in Japan's financial system and the slowdown in its economy will become. Banks will have less capital, and therefore less money to lend.

Japan faces the prospect of zero or even negative real GNP

growth for at least two years. There will be pain but, even more important, there will be shock. The downturn will appear calamitous to the Japanese, since it will be the first time such an extended economic slowdown has occurred since 1945. There will also be the drama of a banking crisis to increase the general level of angst. The competence of the bureaucracy and of the ruling political order will be questioned and changes will be implemented, not out of moral outrage, but for the practical reason that the old way of doing things will no longer seem to work. As a result, more thorough deregulation of the domestic economy will occur, be it the land market, retailing laws, or the domestic distribution system. This will help to reduce tensions with America and other trading partners by promoting internal consumption and reducing the dependence on capital investment. This in turn will mean that in future, domestic economic growth will not be distorted in the way that produced the swollen economic bubble of the 1980s. Such reforms will complement a change of focus in the political system, which will finally begin to do a better job of representing the interests of the salaried middle class, the people who made the economic miracle possible in the first place.

# Epilogue

Much of what is warned about in this book became the subject of headline news in the first half of 1992. But not all of it. For the big issue that confronts Japan has become even more strikingly apparent. This is the extent to which market pressures stemming from Japan's financial crunch will force the country to adopt a form of capitalism more in line with the Western model, with all the political consequences that implies for changes in the way Japan is governed.

It is already clear that Japan's establishment, the tight nexus of businessmen, bureaucrats, financiers, and politicians, has suffered its biggest shock since 1945 as a result of the bursting of the Bubble Economy. Nor is the trauma over yet. Certainly the daily march of events in the first half of 1992 brought little relief from the building momentum of recessionary forces. The economy continued to slow and capital spending to be slashed. In March industrial production fell 5.6 percent year-on-year, and the amount of overtime worked in manufacturing companies plummeted 20 percent. The same month Japanese department-store sales fell 4.1 percent year-on-year. This was the first such decline ever recorded, excluding the months affected by the introduction of the controversial consumption tax in 1989. Companies from Hitachi and Fujitsu down, seeking to cut costs, announced they were freezing the salaries of all staff at kacho level and above. *Kacho*, as section advisers or the equivalent of middle management in the West, represent the commander corps of the Japanese industrial machine. The same deceleration was confirmed by the monetary data. Money supply grew by just 1.6 percent year-on-year in April, yet another all-time low.

Faced with the near-universal evidence of slowdown, policy-makers have found their disagreements more acute. Calls for and expectations of a stimulatory supplementary budget in the second half of 1992 have mounted even as the finance ministry has adhered to its official line that economic demand will revive naturally by the autumn. The optimists have in their favor some seemingly powerful reasons for complacency. After all, Japan enjoys virtually full employment, inflation is running at under 2 percent, and the government has enough fiscal leeway to boost the economy, if it wants to, via an expansionist budget.

Yet behind the dry economic data lies a starker message. The economy has begun to converge with the sorry state of the Tokyo stock market, which is now into the third year of a brutal bear market that still shows little sign of having reached its nadir. In March the Nikkei index crashed below the psychologically key 20,000 level in a dramatic fashion that captured the world's attention, even prompting hearings in the American Senate; the stock market then kept on falling until the Nikkei bounced off 16,500 in April, nearly 60 percent below its all-time high. The plunge marked the stock market's unimpressed response to a combined fiscal and monetary easing announced on March 31 and April 1, despite the fact that the Bank of Japan's cut in the official discount rate from 4.5 percent to 3.75 percent was unexpectedly large, given the continued tough anti-inflationary talk emanating from the central bank. There was also no doubt as to which sector suffered the brunt of the selling: It was the banks. Investors belatedly delivered their judgment on the prospects for that industry. It was crushing. On April 9 the Nikkei index closed at 16,598, or 57 percent lower than where it stood at the end of 1989, marking a loss of wealth of more than $2 trillion. The final plunge occurred between March 31 and

loans off and sell collateral, further depressing land values. In claiming that this strategy is a viable one, bankers and bureaucrats always cite American banks' management of the third world debt crisis as the example they wish to emulate. They forget, though, that this problem was only resolved when debts began to be marked to market and after at least five years of booming asset growth in the 1980s had boosted American (and other) banks' profits. (A large chunk of these profits, of course, came from making loans that subsequently turned sour, be it loans to credit-card carrying consumers or to overeager property developers.) By contrast, Japanese bank lending is now barely growing, itself the consequence of banks' ravaged capital, while the value of the assets that form the collateral of the banking system is still falling, in what remains essentially a deflationary environment.

Whether Japanese banks pull off this hold-and-wait strategy will be touch and go, for, crucially and perhaps improbably, it depends on none of them breaking ranks by starting to dump collateral. One point is clear: At best, bank profits and (because of a protracted period of weak loan growth) economic activity will be depressed for several years by the burden of carrying the dead weight of this bad debt. Also, the cost of capital to Japanese companies will rise markedly as the banks charge solvent borrowers more to help pay for those bad debts. This will be the long-term cost Japan will have to bear, both for not having a system of sound prudential regulation where bad loans are owned up to and reserved against, and for not having an established corporate bond market in place ready to take up the slack. Such a market, however, should now develop fast.

The famous Japanese ways for resolving problems also are coming under increasingly visible strain as the financial squeeze intensifies. One example is the main bank system. In the two major bank rescues announced to date the authorities have had to get a number of banks to share in the cost of the bailouts because no one main bank would agree to shoulder all the pain. This is a sign of weakness, not strength, given the way the system is supposed to work. In the case of the long-awaited bailout of Toyo

Shinkin, which was finally announced in May 1992 after months of negotiations with recalcitrant creditors, finance ministry officials made IBJ bear most of the burden even though Toyo Shinkin is part of the Sanwa Bank group. Sanwa evidently refused to accept sole responsibility for the mess, and its obduracy paid off. IBJ, however, suffered heavily for its financing of Onoue since it was viewed by the authorities, quite reasonably, as the criminal's main bank. It had to forgive 70 percent of its loans to Toyo Shinkin, taking a hit of some ¥11 billion. Its nonbank affiliate, IBJ Lease, also had to forgive 42 percent of the larger sum Toyo Shinkin owes it. In a second bank rescue announced in May Taiheyo Bank, a smallish Tokyo bank, was bailed out by no less than four city banks. The key point here is that the finance ministry could not persuade one bank to take over the business, which clearly would have been preferable. This bailout followed the usual pattern of the growing number of reschedulings that have been announced, be they of property companies or nonbanks. Interest rates charged on outstanding debt were reduced to below-market levels and property was put up for sale.

As the main bank system creaks under the strain the stock market's continuing problems provide evidence that Japan's cozy system of cross-shareholdings has started to unravel. This is natural since fewer and fewer cross-shareholdings are earning their keep in terms of generating business revenues. While viewed simply as an investment, dividends paid are meager and capital losses have been piling up. The best example remains bank shares because so many companies own them for reasons of long-standing relationships. It is now finally dawning on such companies that their bank shares provide them with virtually no income, are probably unnecessary from a relationship point of view, and can be rather costly given the 80 percent plunge in bank share prices already suffered from top to bottom.

The decline in Japanese land and share prices and the unraveling of cross-shareholdings have another significance. They provide the best opportunity in many years for foreign companies to set up, expand, or buy businesses in the world's second largest market.

The authorities in Tokyo will hardly be able to object to such a development since Japanese companies have made so many direct investments overseas in recent years. Indeed, Japanese companies' cumulative direct investments overseas at the end of 1990 were twenty times greater than foreign companies' direct investments in Japan. Japanese share prices may well become really cheap in a final cathartic panic-driven dumping of shares, since this is the way most great bear markets end. But at their April 1992 lows it is fair to say that Japanese shares are approaching relative fair value, at least compared with the ludicrous extremes they reached at the end of 1989 and even compared with the dizzy levels prevailing on Wall Street in the early summer of 1992. Certainly the lower the Tokyo stock market falls the keener cash-strapped Japanese sellers will become and the sweeter the deals will look to foreign buyers.

Sales of cross-shareholdings, especially bank shares, will also be brought on by companies' own financial difficulties. One company that wants to sell its bank shareholdings is Yamatane Securities, which admittedly has peculiar problems. It found itself embroiled in yet another form of securities scandal, which erupted in February and which, in terms of the losses sustained by stock-broking firms, managed to shock even the by now extremely jaded souls inhabiting Japan's securities markets. The problem here was an upside-down Japanese version of pass-the-parcel known as *tobashi*, which literally means to hurl something. Always keener than most to admit that an investment or a loan has gone wrong, the Japanese have perfected ways of getting underwater securities holdings at least temporarily into other hands when end-year balance sheets are drawn up. The issue first surfaced in February when Cosmo Securities, a medium-sized securities firm, announced that it had agreed to pay ¥41.5 billion in an out-of-court settlement to Skylark, a restaurant chain. (Yamatane lost ¥19.5 billion from similar *tobashi* trades.) The details of this scam are revealing. At issue was a repurchase agreement that fell through. It has long been entrenched practice in Japan for company A, facing a loss on an investment, to move it to company B with a different financial year-end, on the understanding that company A will buy it back, paying company B an agreed amount of "interest" for the service rendered. A securities firm, acting as an intermediary, will usually guarantee such agreements. In the Cosmo case a salesman manager at the securities firm needed to raise cash to compensate corporate clients for losses on their share portfolios. He obtained the money by persuading Skylark in July 1991 (note, after the loss-compensation scandal first surfaced) to pay ¥41 billion for American zero-coupon bonds, which were then worth only some ¥5 billion. (Zeros are used because they are unlisted securities in Japan and so their price can be more easily manipulated.) In this case Skylark was promised a profit of ¥2 billion on the transaction. The problem occurred when an unnamed third party, which had promised to buy back the bonds presumably for another fee, refused to do so. Cosmo evidently tried to back out of its agreement and Skylark went to court. The result was that Cosmo had to pay up, suffering a net loss of ¥36 billion on the transaction, a hit that amounted to one-third of its capital.

Yet the Cosmo case seemed relatively small beer compared with the *tobashi* bombshell that exploded the next month when Daiwa, Japan's second biggest securities firm, announced that it would pay ¥73.5 billion to settle lawsuits brought by five companies, all of which concerned *tobashi*. Daiwa's president, Masahiro Dozen, resigned amidst a blaze of publicity (as had Cosmo's chairman). Yet there was something new about these latest scandals. They were settled in a most untypically Japanese manner—via formal lawsuits. This was evidence that the previous summer's scandals had made a difference in one important respect: Loss compensation was now an illegal act. Disgruntled investors were therefore in a more powerful position to seek legal redress against brokers that let them down. The Daiwa case also lent credibility to persistent rumors that securities firms faced liabilities running into trillions of yen, as a result of lawsuits arising from *tobashi*-style repurchase agreements. To date, no more big losses have been made public. They may never be, because the Cosmo and Daiwa examples have given other securities companies every incentive to try to settle these disputes privately, outside the law courts, in which case no one need ever know about them.

The same attempts to avoid taking losses have also been unearthed in the property world. A program on the usually rather tame state-owned television channel NHK detailed shenanigans carried out by Mitsui Trust, Japan's oldest trust bank, which also has the misfortune to be the main bank and so main lender to Azabu Building, the major bubble developer whose flamboyant chairman Kitaro Watanabe was the nearest thing Japan's speculative boom produced to a Donald Trump. As part of its effort to stave off Azabu's insolvency, Mitsui Trust, which had installed its own management team to run the company, announced that nearly ¥300 billion of the company's Tokyo properties would be sold off. Buyers were evidently hard to find. The NHK program detailed Mitsui Trust's adventure in what the reporter described, appropriately, as "land *tobashi.*" It showed how Azabu had sold a property in Tokyo well above its market value to a certain company. The reporter tried to locate this company at its registered address but found no sign of it. Listed as directors of the paper company were employees of Mitsui Trust.

Still, as the habitual weaving and dodging continues, there are some refreshing signs that Japanese officials are beginning to discuss problems frankly, at least when they are outside Japan. An example is a speech given in May 1992 by Masashi Yumoto, managing director of the Tokyo Stock Exchange, at London's Chatham House. Yumoto did not put his audience to sleep with the usual platitudes customary for such occasions. Rather, he declared bluntly that "for the first time in the history of postwar Japan, the safety and soundness of the financial system itself has been questioned," adding that "reliance on the oral guidance of the Ministry of Finance is to be stopped." Noting correctly that the almost unanimous consensus of prominent economists was that the economy would pick up in the second half of 1992, Yumoto also conceded that the stock market remained "somewhat unconvinced."

These are extraordinarily frank comments for a senior Japanese official, even if they were articulated outside Japan. They also reflect a healthy phenomenon—namely that leading representatives of the system are finally addressing the problems. The same

[203]

process of questioning long-held assumptions has begun in the corporate sphere. Japanese companies are beginning to realize that they have reached the limits of the expansionist industrial strategy they have pursued globally since the 1950s. As a consequence, they are starting to turn away from their obsessive pursuit of global market share to a more Western-style stress on profitability and return on equity. The change will have a profound effect on how Japan manages itself. It also will be accelerated by the worse-than-expected economic slowdown. Japanese companies have begun to realize that there is a practical limit to the pursuit of market share. Quite apart from the political constraints posed by the ever-present threat of a protectionist backlash, there also are sound commercial reasons for changing course. Easy money in the late 1980s led to wasteful spending, diseconomies of scale, and a proliferation of products that now clog Japan's warehouses. Warehouse and transport expenses, for example, make up 9 percent of companies' total production costs in Japan, twice the level of America. It is estimated that if Hitachi were to reduce its research-and-development spending to 1988 levels as a proportion of sales (still double that of 1982) its pretax profits would double. The results of this excess are now being paid for in the third consecutive year of declining corporate profitability. For companies have substantially raised their break-even point as a consequence of the capital spending binge. That means that if their sales decline their profits collapse. Tetsuo Tsukimura, an economist at Smith Barney, an American securities firm, notes that the problems now confronting Japanese companies are not the result of external shocks but rather are largely of their own creation. He writes: "The capital they have invested in recent years simply can no longer sustain its own value. Companies gravely misjudged prospective demand conditions and, as a result, are now saddled with the burden of excess production capacity and redundant labor. Companies have little choice but to make adjustments in the area of personnel expenses. Salary freezes, of course, are but the first step."

This raises the multitrillion yen question of whether companies' need to cut costs and boost profits will mark the end of Japan's

post-1945 era of victimless capitalism. Will major Japanese companies start laying off their own employees? Japanese companies will
always be at a competitive disadvantage with their foreign rivals if
they have to carry such fixed overhead without the option of
redundancies.

The right to fire has yet to be articulated by any major Japanese businessman. But the logical path to that way of thinking, in
terms of the need to put profits first and so have the flexibility to
cut costs in response to the ups and downs of the business cycle,
has been articulated by Sony chairman Akio Morita in a widely
hailed article that appeared in the January 1992 issue of the highly
respected monthly publication *Bugei Shunju.* In a speech given in
Honolulu the same month Morita repeated the same message.
Stating that Japan needs a new "paradigm" for competitiveness,
Morita said, "Japan's corporations have, in many cases, sacrificed
potential and legitimate profits in an effort to secure a strong place
in the market, taking razor-thin profit margins which no Western
company would be able to tolerate.

"Now, by and large this does not violate the rules of competition, but it surely fails to embrace the spirit of competition
found in the United States and Europe. And often it is not only
the employees and shareholders who must bear the brunt of this
strategy, but smaller suppliers and subcontractors are also forced
to face hardships. It comes as no surprise, then, that foreign competitors sometimes feel threatened by what they find to be a different Japanese approach to competition. This is because they do
not have the luxury of a sacrificing labor force and low dividend
outlays."

Morita went on to advocate a new corporate philosophy of
management, noting in his *Bungei Shunju* article that Japanese
companies should be aware that "European and American toler-
ance of Japanese business practices is reaching its limit." The new
philosophy as described by Morita means more stress on raising
profits and higher dividend pay-out ratios. It also means seeking to
boost employees' "quality of life" through such measures as longer
holidays and even higher salaries. Japan must adopt an approach

"which gives greater priority to the freedom of each individual member of a company than to a victory in the market place."

Naturally, there is no shortage of foreign skeptics ready to scoff at Morita's rhetoric. The view of many is that his remarks are special pleadings designed to stave off protectionist pressures and that it will be back to business as usual in terms of exclusive pursuit of market share as Japan once again exports its way out of its problems. After all, it is the credo of the so-called "revisionists" that in Japan, to quote their favorite battle cry, "nothing ever changes." These people will be proved wrong because market pressures caused by the bursting of the Bubble Economy will force Japanese companies to make these changes if they wish to continue to prosper. Morita, a brilliant self-made businessman, understands this instinctively. Those Japanese companies that make the strategic change first will be those that will emerge the strongest in the new era. Indeed, there is already growing anecdotal evidence of just such a change in corporate behavior. The car and electronics industries, for example, employ more than a quarter of Japan's work force and account for nearly 30 percent of capital investment in manufacturing. In America Japanese carmakers have begun to raise prices to an extent that suggests both that they hope to appease protectionist pressures and that they are starting to put profits before further gains in market share. Matsushita, the consumer electronics giant, has announced it plans to cut its domestic range of 50,000 products by 20,000 in a bid both to cut costs and relieve a confused and satiated customer.

It also should not be assumed that the adoption of a more Western-style approach would mark an entirely new direction for Japan. It would not. Japan has had orthodox capitalists before. In fact, both lifetime employment and the obsessive focus on market share are largely post-1945 inventions. As recently as the 1920s Japan pursued a neoclassical policy remarkable for its "orthodoxy" as the economy was deflated with the specific purpose of putting the country back on the gold standard. The stresses this put on the economy, and subsequently on the body politic with the resulting rise of militarism, are described in a Cornell University paper entitled "Convergence and Its Costs: The International Politics of Japanese Macroeconomic Liberalisation, 1918–1932" by David Asher, now a congressional aide resident in Japan. Asher quotes a remark made by a former Bank of Japan governor and finance minister, Junnosuke Inoue, the key architect of this deflationary policy, in a 1926 lecture delivered to bankers in Kyoto. "It is as dangerous to transgress economic laws as it is to transgress the laws of nature. The pendulum which controls the economic mechanism of the world has its fixed limits of travel. . . . Tamper with that pendulum, force it beyond those limits, and it will only swing back and smite you. . . . The principles of economics never vary, but between them there is always the human element with all its powers for good and evil."

Here indeed was a champion of free-market forces, of the natural cyclical laws of economics, a man who, as Asher notes, viewed Japan "in anything but 'unique' or nationalist terms," a man who postulated that its economy should be subjected to the "same natural economic forces as the rest of the civilized world." Likewise, the liberal internationalist-minded Inoue was a committed free trader. He wrote in his 1931 book, *Problems of the Japanese Exchange*, "Now let us hear what the consumer has to say. Higher tariff barriers mean nothing more or less than higher prices for him to pay. We all eat rice, we all eat barley, and every meal which we eat is taxed. All very well for the Ministry of Finance who gets the taxes, but less so for the consumer, for whom this means an intolerable burden."

These commendable sentiments would be music to the ears of modern-day American trade negotiators. However, the reality of Inoue's policies as finance minister were intensely deflationary for the economy during the period. With the world already reeling from the 1929 Wall Street panic Japan lifted the gold embargo at the old parity in January 1930. The result was to sink the country into the most severe depression in modern history. Takafusa Nakamura, a distinguished economic historian, describes the impact in his chapter on the period in *The Cambridge History of Japan.* "The countryside reeled under the sudden drop in the prices of key commodities such as rice and silk cocoons. There were many instances reported of salary payments for village primary schoolteachers being postponed for half a year due to shortfalls in local tax revenues, and of increases in the number of homes that had their electricity cut off. In metropolitan areas the number of unemployed grew, and the majority of recent university graduates were unable to find work." Yet despite such visible social distress the government, determined to maintain the gold standard, did not relent and continued to follow a policy of fiscal and monetary austerity. The deflationary result was that by 1931 export prices had fallen to 40 percent and the gross national expenditure deflator to 73 percent of their respective 1929 levels, according to Nakamura. The social unrest mounted. On September 18, 1931, the Manchurian incident occurred as the military signaled it was ready to begin pursuing its own expansionist agenda. On September 23 Britain went off the gold standard. On December 13 the Japanese government finally collapsed, unrelenting to the end. A new government was formed and the same day gold was re-embargoed and payments of specie were suspended. Japan was off the gold standard, probably forever. Tariffs were subsequently raised, and the country followed a policy of boosting exports via a devalued currency. On May 15, 1932, in the midst of an election campaign, Inoue was assassinated by farm village youths from Ibaraki Prefecture. They were members of the nationalist Ketsumeidan, or Blood League. A few weeks later the same extremist group assassinated Takuma Dan, head of the Mitsui *zaibatsu*, which had suffered popular resentment for speculating profitably against the yen prior to the move off the gold standard.

It is not necessary to postulate a return to the neoclassical economic orthodoxy practiced by Inoue to make the point that the corporatist management of the economy that has prevailed in Japan since 1945 has not always done so; that the country is not culturally programmed in some mysterious way to manage its affairs in this fashion. Moreover, the two leading political parties of the 1920s prior to the rise of militarism also illuminate how the LDP might splinter ideologically in response to an economic crisis. Inoue's political party, the Minseito, of which he was the leader when he was killed, favored fiscal balance, free trade, and general pre-Keynesian orthodoxy. Its opponent, the Seiykai, supported public spending on infrastructure, subsidies and tariffs, and the rest of the policies usually associated with managed economies. Now consider this divide in the modern context. The policy that has been pursued by the Bank of Japan under the Mieno regime is highly orthodox in its deflationary rigor. Likewise, there is no shortage of descendants of the Seiyukai in the LDP, who would like Japan to deficit spend its way out of the current recession. Thus Kanemaru, the LDP's crusty political godfather, called publicly in early June for a ¥7-8 trillion supplementary budget, far higher than most economists' estimates, before leaving to see President George Bush in Washington. The move was designed both to put pressure on the finance ministry and to please Bush, who naturally favors pro-growth policies in a presidential election year. Earlier in the year Kanemaru had also made waves when he demanded publicly that the Bank of Japan cut interest rates more aggressively, even if this meant sacking Mieno.

These parallels are worth making. For there are plenty of signs that Japan has again entered a period of convergence with the West, just as it did in the 1920s, as the country is urged by Morita and other influential spokesmen to behave more like a market economy; to stop pursuing a narrowly focused nationalist agenda predicated on Japan's supposed differences and vulnerabilities. This internationalist trend can only be furthered by any foreign buying of Japanese corporate and physical assets at distressed prices since it will increase foreign ownership and therefore influence in the Japanese economy. The concern is that convergence will generate the same sort of backlash among more traditional and reactionary elements of society that led to the political assassinations and military adventurism of the 1930s and 1940s. It is not necessary to predict a repeat of such calamities, and hopefully the forces of internationalism will triumph this time, to point out that the domestic impact of the collapse of the Bubble Economy could be as profound economically, politically, and socially as it has already manifestly been financially. The continuation of the post-1945 order undisturbed cannot be assumed. Indeed, for its own good, Japan needs to advance on all three fronts. The economy, as presently structured, has reached its commercial limits. The political system is moribund to the point of paralysis and the social order is positively backward in terms of its distrust of individual initiative.

David Hale, an international economist with Chicago-based Kemper Financial Services, wrote in a 1992 paper on the Tokyo stock-market crash that during the 1980s the interaction of Japan's supereasy monetary policy with its system of banking and securities cartels caused the country to evolve "from financial barbarism to decadence" without passing through any intervening period of capitalist restructuring that would be recognizable in America. The crash signals the transition to an era in which capital will be more expensive and savings will be allocated for investment by freer markets in debt and equity, and not just by banks. Hale notes correctly that such a freer market should encourage more Japanese convergence with Western capitalism. The great unresolved question for Japan and its trade competitors is how much. It is the contention here that Japan will converge substantially with the West, though naturally it will do so in its own fashion, and that the convergence will occur quicker than most expect, precisely because of the intensity of the economic slowdown, the shocks to the existing system that it will pose, and the market pressures that it will unleash in terms of the need for radical change.

That Japan will converge is positive for its trade competitors and also for the Japanese consumer. A country that has had a persistent trade and current account surplus with the rest of the world for a quarter of a century is a country that chronically underconsumes. Japan will have its supply-side shock. And the country should emerge from its current distress a fully signed-up member of the international community, heart, head, and maybe even soul.

TOKYO, JUNE 1992